Becoming a
Multiple Intelligences
School

Thomas R. Hoerr

ASCD

Association for Supervision and Curriculum Development
Alexandria, Virginia   USA

ASCD®

Association for Supervision and Curriculum Development
1703 N. Beauregard St. • Alexandria, VA 22311-1714 USA
Telephone: 1-800-933-2723 or 703-578-9600 • Fax: 703-575-5400
Web site: http://www.ascd.org • E-mail: member@ascd.org

Printed in the United States of America.

s 2/2000

ASCD Stock No. 100006
ASCD member price: $19.95   nonmember price: $23.95

Library of Congress Cataloging-in-Publication Data
Hoerr, Thomas R., 1945-
     Becoming a multiple intelligences school / Thomas R. Hoerr.
          p. cm.
Includes bibliographical references and index.
"ASCD stock no. 100006."
     ISBN 0-87120-365-0
   1. Multiple intelligences—Case studies.   2. Cognitive styles in children—Case studies.   3. New City School (Saint Louis, Mo.)
4. Curriculum planning—Case studies. I. Title.
     LB1060 .H62 2000
        370.15'2—dc21   99-050514

06   05   04   03   02   01   00   10 9 8 7 6 5 4 3 2 1

BECOMING
A MULTIPLE INTELLIGENCES
SCHOOL

FOREWORD

We would all love to remake ourselves, or our worlds, over a long weekend. Perhaps that is why there is a perennial market for self-improvement books about weight and appearance and a continuous demand for three-day seminars that promise greater creativity, a richer spiritual life, or the transformation of schools.

In life, however, miracles are few. If one seeks fundamental changes, one is better off heeding Winston Churchill who, during the battle of Britain, promised his countrymen nothing but "blood, toil, tears, and sweat." Educational systems that are truly impressive, such as the preschools of Reggio Emilia, Italy, or the selective liberal arts colleges of New England, achieve their status over decades; moreover, they devote enormous energy and resources simply to maintaining their distinctive edge.

Flavor-of-the-month slogans or manipulations have little to do with genuine educational change. I include in this characterization the set of educational ideas with which I am most closely associated—the theory of multiple intelligences (MI theory). While appealing on the surface to many educators, the application of MI theory to schools is a process that does not permit quick fixes. The effort to take the differences among individuals seriously, and to recast curriculum, instruction, and assessment in light of those differences, requires significant teamwork over several years. One learns the most from schools that have explored the educational implications of MI theory for more than a decade, such as the Key Learning Community in Indianapolis.

In this invaluable book, Tom Hoerr relates a decade's worth of MI experiences at St. Louis's New City School. We learn about the staff's initial exposure to MI theory; the many activities (some more successful than others) that were undertaken by faculty and staff in teaching, curriculum, adult development, and assessment; and the challenges that the leader faces in attempting to bring about significant and lasting change. Especially compelling are the continuing efforts to develop the personal intelligences during a period when issues of diversity, multiculturalism, and standards loom so large.

I learned much from this book. Hoerr underscores the centrality of collegiality, the problems posed by transient students and faculty, the complementary role played by public exhibitions and standardized test scores, the role of friends in determining the activities (and intelligences) favored by children, the delicate line between support and challenge that the leader must walk, the tension between excellence and perfection. I value the concrete examples, as well as the ties to important conceptual work, such as that undertaken by Roland Barth on collegiality,

Peter Salovey on emotional intelligence, and Peter Senge on the learning organization.

Achieving excellence has always been a process. Hoerr makes it abundantly clear that the effort to use MI ideas effectively must remain on the agenda. Still, I can testify that, over a 10-year period, clear, palpable, impressive progress can be made. We can improve schools significantly, but only if we take the long view and do not settle for patchwork fixes. Reading about the struggles and victories of the New City School family, I was reminded of another memorable remark of Winston Churchill's: "This is not the end. It is not even the beginning of the end. But it is, perhaps, the end of the beginning."

HOWARD GARDNER
CAMBRIDGE, MA

PREFACE

The New City School is an independent school in the city of St. Louis, Missouri, serving 360 students from three years old through the 6th grade. The schoolhouse is turn-of-the-century, originally built as an all-girls day school, elementary through high school. We make good use of our space, with wooden lofts built in most classrooms to take advantage of the high ceilings. Giant concrete sculptures sit on our lawns—a huge frog, turtle, and serpents—telling everyone who passes by that this is not a typical school! An eight-foot-tall, multi-headed papier-mâché dragon greets everyone just inside the front door, each head corresponding to one of the original multiple intelligences. For example, one head wears giant reading glasses while another has a coach's whistle. Once inside the building, visitors walk through halls adorned with students' work reflecting their use all of the intelligences.

New City School opened its doors in 1969, created by neighbors who wanted a school to be an anchor and stem the disinvestment of property values. In some respects, New City has succeeded in this mission and is credited by many as a key factor in the revitalization of St. Louis's central west end. Yet St. Louis still struggles with many of the poverty issues facing all major cities. Five hundred yards directly south of New City are renovated mansions built in the early 1900s, worth hundreds of thousands of dollars; 500 yards to the north are boarded up apartment buildings and vacant lots.

Beginning with 100 children, New City has grown to be the largest independent elementary school in St. Louis. The school was founded on the premise that children learn best when they learn with those who are both similar to and different from themselves, and this thrust for diversity continues today. During the 1999–2000 school year, 33 percent of our students are minorities (mostly African American); 26.7 percent of our student body, students of all races, receive need-based financial aid; and students are enrolled from 50 zip codes, representing nearly all of the St. Louis metropolitan area, although a majority of students live in the city of St. Louis. Although an independent school, New City's enrollment policies are quite inclusive. Space permitting, the overwhelming majority of the students who apply to New City are admitted. We do not seek to enroll the "best and brightest."

Because we are an independent school, we have some advantages not often available to public schools. Our class sizes average 17:1 in grades 1–6 and parents choose us based on our mission. Although we are inclusive in our admissions policies, we do not get a cross-section of students; families choose us because they value education and that is an incredible advantage.

We accept the challenges of being an independent school, too. Each year parents decide whether we are truly worth thousands of dollars of tuition and "vote with their feet" about whether they wish to remain at New City. If we are not meeting their children's needs they will not stay. Parental expectations are increased; parents who pay tuition feel that they have the right to expect more from a school.

Being an independent school means that there is additional pressure placed on our students. Our 6th graders must take competitive tests and go to various secondary schools for personal interviews to determine whether they will be accepted. We help our students view the application and interview process as a learning experience, one that will begin to prepare them for the many applications they will submit throughout their lifetime, but there is no denying the stress for our students and their parents.

ACKNOWLEDGMENTS

I am indebted to many people. First, I cannot begin to express the gratitude I feel toward Howard Gardner. I owe Howard a great deal, not just for his conception of the theory of multiple intelligences, but for his kindness and support.

I owe much to the entire New City School community. Our faculty, as you will gather from reading this book, is exceptional. They are caring, talented, creative, and dedicated. I feel fortunate to work with teachers and administrators who put kids first in everything that they do. Their willingness to search for a better way to help all of our students learn is inspiring. (Plus, they tolerantly and patiently roll their eyes at my bad jokes.) Our students and families are also special. They trust us and care for us in many ways. Education is a partnership and our families walk with us in our efforts to discover new ways to help students learn. The members of the New City Board of Directors deserve special recognition for their commitment to excellence. Years ago they expressed their appreciation of and confidence in me by granting me some time away from school, a minisabbatical, to read, reflect, and think about the future. I read *Frames of Mind* (Gardner, 1983) and life has never been the same for any of us!

On a personal level, much of who I am, the good anyway, is due to the support of my wife, Karleen. She is a woman of many strengths and I have gained much from her. My mother, Rita Curtis, has been unwavering in her confidence in me. Her love and support have made all the difference. I owe much to Pauline Wolff, my former secretary who helped me find a degree of organization amidst the detritus on my desk and in my head. And both John O'Neil and Darcie Russell, my editors at ASCD, warrant much appreciation for their skill and support in helping me turn ideas into readable sentences.

Finally, although she no longer walks this earth, I would be remiss if I did not take a moment to acknowledge my 1st grade teacher, Mrs. Mayfield. At Monroe School, in south St. Louis, Helen Mayfield was everything that a good teacher should be. She believed in me and she pushed me. Whatever scholastic success I have realized started with her. I think of her often.

INTRODUCTION

Great works are performed not by strengths,
but by perseverence.

—Samuel Johnson

All of us want our students to succeed. We chose a career in education and we remain educators in large part because of the satisfaction we derive from making a difference in the life of a youngster. This fundamental motivation to help all students learn has moved teachers and principals to explore multiple intelligences (MI) theory as a tool that makes it possible for more kids to succeed. Too many classrooms are characterized by a pecking order of scholastic winners and losers. MI theory teaches us that all kids are smart, but they are smart in different ways. All children have potential. Teachers and principals are finding that using MI not only increases the opportunities for students to learn, but also gives adults more avenues and ways to grow professionally and personally.

Because MI is neither a curriculum nor a pedagogy, the ways that it can be used in classrooms and schools are as unlimited as the creativity and energies of educators working together. And educators working as colleagues is the key; the chance that MI will flourish in a school increases as teachers work together and learn with and from one another. Indeed, entire schools are embracing MI as their focus. Whether an existing school adopts MI as a focus or a new school frames its program around MI from the beginning, the merit of using MI schoolwide is clear: It has the potential to help children learn and it can create a setting in which adults learn, too.

When a school becomes a true MI school, every aspect of its program and curriculum changes. The approaches vary enormously, but several aspects of school change are associated with all successful MI implementations. First, using MI means moving from working to match and fit students to the existing curriculum to creating new curriculums to meet students' strengths. Using MI also means changing what is assessed and how it is assessed. Paper and pencil tests have their place, to be sure; it is important that students learn how to read, write, and compute. That said, there are many other ways for students to learn and demonstrate what they understand by using the nonscholastic intelligences. When schools incorporate MI, alternative assessment techniques, including portfolios, exhibitions, and presentations, become integral tools for recording and understanding student progress. Finally, in an MI school, relationships with students' parents change: Educators have a greater responsibility to educate their students' parents, and parents are offered more ways to connect to the school.

This is more than a book about how MI can be used in classrooms. It is also a book about leadership. It is a book written for educational leaders of all kinds: principals, assistant principals, curriculum supervisors, central office administrators, aspiring administrators, and university faculty members whose focus is curriculum, instruction, or administration. This book is also written for teacher leaders, those who by dint of their skills, interests, and reputation are looked to by their peers for leadership and counsel, whether or not they have an administrative title.

The New City School faculty has been implementing MI theory since 1988. I believe that we were the second school in the country to do so (preceded by the Key School in Indianapolis). My thoughts stem, certainly, from those years of experience. The New City School faculty—an incredible group of superb teachers from whom I have learned much—has experienced the excitement and satisfaction that comes from breaking new ground and seeing kids grow as a result of our efforts. We have also, however, encountered the frustrations that come from failed attempts and from trying to do too much too soon. In this book, I recount both the highs and lows of our implementation in a way that, I hope, allows you to learn from our successes and our mistakes.

We are all products of our experiences, and this book reflects what I have learned in a range of settings. Before arriving at New City School in 1981, I was the principal of a public elementary school, working with disadvantaged minority youth. Before that, I taught in diverse environments, including a middle-class suburban public school and an inner-city public school located amidst public housing.

Perception is reality; we act on the world that we see. My experiences have caused me to bring certain beliefs to the table, to look at the world through a particular lens. Setting out these biases (at least those of which I am aware) may be helpful to the reader.

• *I believe that all children can learn.* Although this comment is so pervasive that it sounds trite, it is only trite because we often say it, hear it, read it, and write it without reflecting upon or changing our behavior. The reality is that not all children learn. MI theory offers a way to reach those students who have fallen between the cracks, some whose talents do not lie in reading and writing.

• *I believe that a school is no better than the quality of its faculty.* Yes, curriculum is important, as is a safe and comfortable physical setting. But these conditions alone do not mean that students will learn. A strong faculty, one that respects and addresses students' needs, can help students grow and learn. Good teachers make a difference in children's lives.

• *I believe that the role of the principal is to help everyone in the building learn.* It is easy for school administrators to get weighed down in paperwork and student behavior problems. And unfortunately, the ethos of a building may place a premium on student control and teachers working in isolation. Good principals, though, transcend these conditions. They ask hard questions and they listen; they provide support and they listen; they challenge and they listen. They create an environment in which everyone—students, staff, and parents—learns.

The nine chapters in this book cover all aspects of implementing MI theory. Chapter 1 provides an overview of MI theory, defining the intelligences and contrasting MI to traditional notions of intellect. Chapter 2 describes New City School and follows our path to MI. Roland Barth's model of collegiality is covered in Chapter 3; I offer specific suggestions for developing collegiality within a school. Assessment is the focus of Chapter 4, and a variety of alternative techniques are offered. School-wide strategies for implementing MI and ways to look creatively at the school day and school year are the focus of Chapter 5. Much attention is being paid to the concept of emotional intelligence these days, and I address this concept in Chapter 6, which focuses on the personal intelligences.

In the same way that children pass through

developmental phases, organizations travel through fairly predictable stages as they grow and learn. Chapter 7 addresses the changes that take place as MI (and to a degree, any major educational program) is being implemented. Chapter 8 looks at leading a faculty and offers steps that can be taken to help teachers grow. Although this book is written with an MI focus, I believe that most, if not all, of the leadership and management issues apply to schools and organizations everywhere. Finally, Chapter 9 speculates on the future of MI, how it might be implemented over the next decade.

An old saying goes "To learn something, we must first teach it." Like most classroom teachers, I have experienced this phenomenon firsthand in situations ranging from teaching two-digit division to deciding how a board of directors should be organized. Now, having finished this book, I would modify the saying a bit: "To know something, we must first write about it."

Writing this book has been enormously fulfilling for me. It has forced me to reflect on what I have done, what I should have done, and what I should be doing differently. I reflected before, of course, but not at the level of detail and intensity that were required in writing this book. Reading what I have written makes me proud of my efforts and humble about my mistakes. I hope that reading about my experiences helps you to reflect on your efforts and seek new ways to help students learn.

1 | THE THEORY OF MULTIPLE INTELLIGENCES

What began as a theory of intelligence, intended for psychologists, has become a tool that educators around the world seize with enthusiasm. The theory of multiple intelligences (MI) brings a pragmatic approach to how we define intelligence and allows us to use our students' strengths to help them learn. Students who read and write well are still smart, but they are joined by other students who have different talents. Through MI, schools and classrooms become settings in which a variety of skills and abilities can be used to learn and solve problems. Being smart is no longer determined by a score on a test; being smart is determined by how well students learn in a variety of ways.

The History of the Intelligence Quotient (I.Q.)

We, as humans, have a penchant for measuring things. Perhaps the beginning of the modern search for ways to measure intelligence was the creation of the I.Q. test. In Paris in the early 1900s, Alfred Binet was asked to develop an instrument that would identify youngsters who were mentally deficient and in need of extra help. Thus, the first standardized intelligence test was born. Later, other researchers developed the technique of administering a series of questions to children and recording which items could be answered correctly by almost all youngsters, which by most, which by few, and

which by none. The information was used to create a test that would discern students' levels of knowledge, designed so that a score of 100 would indicate an average intelligence. The idea that intelligence could be objectively measured and reported by a single score took hold. Nearly a century later myriad standardized tests are available for a variety of purposes, and they all are based on Binet's premise that a single test can yield a score that captures all of an individual's abilities and potential.

Of course, we know this is nonsense. How could all of an individual's abilities and potential possibly be captured by a single test, much less a single score? Yet many important educational decisions, including whether a student is accepted into a program or a school, are heavily influenced by a single test or a single score. Despite the fact that the misuse of tests and test scores flies in the face of common sense, many people continue to embrace the I.Q. model, assuming that there is one measure that can assess an individual's intelligence.

Misuse and Overuse of I.Q. and Other Standardized Tests

Although standardized tests of various sorts have their roles and can be used with validity in many instances, they are often misused and overused. Misuse and overuse happen because standardized tests are easy to use, cheap, and accepted (indeed, are often expected) by the public.

Group achievement and I.Q. tests are remarkably inexpensive. Students fill in circles to indicate the response they choose and their answer sheets are shipped away for machine scoring. These relatively inexpensive standardized tests are attractive because most schools operate on a tight budget and the public is familiar with standardized testing. Virtually every parent has taken standardized tests, so they expect their children to do the same.

The strength of standardized tests is that they are *reliable*, yielding the same score over time and, thus, are comparable even though administered in different settings and at different times. Their weakness is that they may or may not be *valid*; what they actually measure may be quite different than what they purport to assess. Standardized tests that ask students to use a multiple-choice format to select the best written passage from four samples, for example, may identify a particular skill, but it is not the skill of writing, which can be determined only by asking students to write. Judging students' writing ability by having them identify good writing may be reliable, but it is certainly not valid.

The biggest problem with standardized tests and the I.Q. model, however, is that they measure intelligence narrowly, based on how well the student reads and computes. Only a few of a students' abilities, the "scholastic" intelligences, chiefly the linguistic and logical mathematical, are assessed. Although unfortunate, this tendency to assess only the linguistic and logical-mathematical intelligences is not surprising because for decades schools have focused, sometimes almost exclusively, on the scholastic intelligences. The tendency to focus on scholastic intelligences is compounded by the fact that it is relatively easy to design reliable (if not always valid) paper and pencil tests for assessing reading, writing, and computation. Designing reliable and valid tests to assess students' musical or artistic talents, for example, is much more difficult and surely more expensive.

Because standardized tests are so focused on the scholastic intelligences, they can reasonably predict future success in school. Real-world success, however, encompasses much more than skill in the linguistic and logical-mathematical arenas. Therefore, that same focus means standardized tests offer little useful predictive information about success in life. For too long we have hidden behind "objective" tests, those yielding consistent and reliable results, disregarding the fact that they measure only a piece of the picture. And because we focus our energies on those things we measure, we wind up giving almost all of our attention to the scholastic intelligences, those that are easily measured through multiple-choice tests.

The Multiple Intelligences (MI) Model

Howard Gardner was working at the Boston Veterans Administration Medical Center when he became aware that brain-damaged patients lost different abilities depending upon the location of the injury in the brain. For example, damage to the frontal lobe results in difficulty producing speech that is grammatical, although it does not affect the ability to understand what has been said. In *Frames of Mind* Gardner says, "Other, even more specific linguistic disorders turn out to be linked to particular regions in the brain: these include selective difficulties in repetition, naming, reading, and writing" (1983, p. 51). He notes that some individuals who have experienced significant aphasia (a loss of language) from brain damage can maintain their musical abilities while, conversely, others become disabled musically yet keep basic language skills (p. 118). To Gardner, these differing losses suggest a biological basis for specialized intelligences. Working from the definition that *intelligence is the ability to solve a problem or create a product that is valued in a culture*, Gardner developed a set of criteria to determine what set of skills make up an intelligence.

These criteria are focused on solving problems and creating products; they are based on biological foundations and psychological aspects of intelligence. He suggests that an ability can be considered an intelligence if it can meet a few (not necessarily all) of these criteria:

• It has the potential to be isolated by brain damage. For example, the location of damage to the brain, such as might occur from a stroke, may result in a person losing certain linguistic abilities.

• It is demonstrated by the existence of idiot savants, prodigies, and other exceptional individuals who demonstrate a high level of skill in one area. For example, by observing people who demonstrate extraordinary ability in a single intelligence, we can watch intelligences in relative isolation.

• It has an identifiable core operation or set of operations. Musical intelligence consists of sensitivity to melody, harmony, rhythm, timbre, and musical structure. Linguistic intelligence consists of sensitivity to structure and syntax, vocabulary, rhythm and cadence, and literary tools (e.g., alliteration).

• It has a distinctive developmental history, along with a definable set of expert "end-state" performances. Expert athletes, poets, and salespersons demonstrate these performance characteristics.

• It has an evolutionary history or evolutionary plausibility. Animals exhibit forms of spatial intelligence; birds have musical intelligence.

• It has support from experimental psychological tasks. Tests can indicate how intelligences are discrete or interrelated.

• It has support from psychometric findings. For example, batteries of tests can reveal which intelligences reflect the same underlying factors.

• It has susceptibility to encoding in a symbol system. Codes such as language, maps, numbers, and facial expressions capture components of the various intelligences.

The definition of intelligence that is supported by these criteria—*the ability to solve a problem or create a product that is valued in a society*—is very different from the definition of intelligence implicit in standardized I.Q. and aptitude tests (one based on verbal fluency, wide vocabulary, and computational skills). While the traditional definition of intelligence focuses on inert knowledge and skills that are especially valuable in school, Gardner's definition is far wider. "Creating a product" could encompass transforming a blank canvas into a picture that evokes emotion, or it might mean forming and leading a productive team from a group that couldn't agree on anything. The definition of "solving a problem or creating a product" is a pragmatic one, focusing on *using* an ability in a real-life situation. Applying his criteria resulted in Gardner asserting that there are more intelligences than those relied upon in I.Q. tests and typically valued in school.

Of course, Gardner is not the first person to suggest that there is more than one intelligence. Decades ago, J. P. Guilford created the Structure of Intellect, a model that identified more than 90 different intellectual capacities, and Robert Sternberg has developed the Triarchic Theory of Intelligence, which contains three forms of intelligence. Recently, Daniel Goleman's *Emotional Intelligence* and Robert Coles's *Moral Intelligence* have received national attention. All of these theories share the belief that intelligence is a multifaceted, complex capacity. Gardner's model is distinguished from the other theories by its breadth, its scientific basis, and its educational implications. Gardner's multiple intelligences are shown in Figure 1.1.*

---

*The naturalist intelligence was not identified in *Frames of Mind,* but was proposed in the 1990s by Gardner. Gardner has speculated that an existential intelligence might be identified as a ninth intelligence.

FIGURE 1.1
Gardner's Multiple Intelligences

Intelligence	Definition	People who exhibit this intelligence
linguistic	sensitivity to the meaning and order of words	Winston Churchill, Doris Kearns Goodwin, Barbara Jordan
logical-mathematical	the ability to handle chains of reasoning and to recognize patterns and order	Bill Gates, Stephen Hawking, Benjamin Banneker
musical	sensitivity to pitch, melody, rhythm and tone	Ray Charles, Harry Connick Jr., Carly Simon
bodily-kinesthetic	the ability to use the body skillfully and handle objects adroitly	Mia Hamm, Michael Jordan, Michelle Kwan
spatial	the ability to perceive the world accurately and to recreate or transform aspects of that world	Mary Engelbreit, Maya Lin, Frank Lloyd Wright
naturalist	the ability to recognize and classify the numerous species, the flora and fauna, of an environment	Charles Darwin, Jane Goodall, George Meriwether Lewis
interpersonal	the ability to understand people and relationships	Colin Powell, Martin Luther King Jr., Deborah Tannen
intrapersonal	access to one's emotional life as a means to understand oneself and others	Anne Frank, Bill Moyers, Eleanor Roosevelt

MI in Schools

Gardner's theory of multiple intelligences resonates so strongly for many educators because it offers a model for acting on what we believe: *all children have strengths*. Many of us were taught to focus on the curriculum as we planned and taught, to concentrate on helping students respond to the curriculum; MI, however, is a student-centered model in which the curriculum is often modified to fit the students. Rather than relying upon a linguistic filter and requiring students to write to show their grasp of skills and information, teachers using MI can allow students to use their strengths to demonstrate what they have learned. Students might use their spatial intelligence in drawing, their musical intelligence in composing a song or identifying a melody, or their bodily-kinesthetic intelligence in acting out an interaction or creating a diorama. Figure 1.2 suggests some possible ways that teachers and students can incorporate the intelligences in teaching and learning.

There is no one, right way to implement MI. That there is no single path to implementation is one of the model's attractions, but also one of its liabilities. The way MI is used at New City School, for example, is different from the way it is used at the Key School in Indianapolis, Indiana, which is different from the way it is brought to life at the Fuller School in Gloucester, Massachusetts. The beauty of this is that each teacher or, preferably, each group of teachers, can use MI in a way that reflects their school's unique context and culture. At the New City School, for example, we believe that the personal intelligences are the most important; at the Key School, however, all intelligences are valued equally. Latitude in implementation respects the professionalism of teachers and trusts their judgment to know how best to meet their students' needs.

Latitude also means, however, that it is possible to *mis*apply MI. Gardner has written with concern about teachers who have music playing in the background and believe that they are addressing the musical intelligence, or teachers who allow students to crawl on the floor during math, thinking that they are addressing the bodily-kinesthetic intelligence. MI can be a powerful tool for reaching students, but using it effectively requires teachers to devote the time and energy to understand MI theory and then decide how it can be used in curriculum development, instruction, and assessment.

At New City School, the MI model has caused us to look differently at curriculum, instruction, and assessment; how we work with parents; and how we work with each other. A good beginning is to explore to what degree you are bringing the different intelligences to life in your classroom. Assess your baseline using the MI Inventory in Appendix A. Share the inventory with colleagues and discuss your results.

✦ ✦ ✦

For Faculty Discussion

1. Which intelligences might have been more valuable in our culture 100 years ago? Which intelligences would have likely been most prized where we live 500 years ago?
2. Looking ahead, how might technology make some of the intelligences more or less important or obsolete?
3. Can we identify former students who were not successful in school but have been successful in life? Can we explain what accounts for this?
4. Why might it be difficult to incorporate many of the intelligences into curriculum and instruction?

FIGURE 1.2
Identifying and Encouraging the Use of Multiple Intelligences in Schools

Intelligence	Students who like to do these activities are often exhibiting their strongest intelligences	To help students develop a particular intelligence, teachers can
linguistic	write stories and essays; tell jokes, stories, puns; use an expanded vocabulary; play word games; use words to create images	encourage the use of outrageous words, and palindromes; involve students in debates and making oral presentations; show how poetry can convey emotion
logical-mathematical	work with numbers, figure things out, analyze situations; see how things work; exhibit precision in problem solving; work in situations with clear answers	use Venn diagrams to compare and contrast; use graphs, tables, and time lines; have students demonstrate using concrete objects; ask students to show sequences
musical	listen to and play music; match feelings to music and rhythm; sing and hum; create and replicate tunes	rewrite song lyrics to teach a concept; encourage students to add music to plays; create musical mnemonics; teach history and geography through the music of the period and place
bodily-kinesthetic	play sports and be physically active; engage in risk taking with their bodies; dance, act, and mime; engage in crafts and play with mechanical objects	provide tactile and movement activities; offer role-playing and acting opportunities; allow students to move while working; use sewing, model making and other activities that require fine motor skills
spatial	doodle, paint or draw; create three-dimensional representations; look at and create maps and diagrams; take things apart and put them back together	draw maps and mazes; lead visualization activities; teach mind mapping; provide opportunities to show understanding through drawing; have students design buildings, clothing, scenery to depict an event or period
naturalist	spend time outdoors; collect plants, rocks, animals; listen to outdoor sounds; notice relationships in nature; classify flora and fauna	use outdoors as a classroom; have plants and animals in the classroom for which students are responsible; conduct hands-on experiments; create a nature area on the playground

FIGURE 1.2—*continued*
Identifying and Encouraging the Use of Multiple Intelligences in Schools

interpersonal	enjoy many friends; lead, share, mediate; build consensus; help others with their problems; be an effective team member	use cooperative learning; assign group projects; give students opportunities for peer teaching; brainstorm solutions; create situations in which students observe and give feedback to others
intrapersonal	reflect; control own feelings and moods; pursue personal interests and set individual agendas; learn through observing and listening; use metacognitive skills	allow students to work at their own pace; create quiet areas within the room or allow students to go outside to work alone; help students set and monitor personal goals; provide opportunities for students to give and receive feedback; involve students in writing journals

(Adapted from *Succeeding with Multiple Intelligences*, by the New City School faculty, 1996.)

A PARADIGM SHIFT

Over a century ago, in *Uncle Tom's Cabin*, Harriet Beecher Stowe presented racial issues in a way that caused a nation to pause. In 1859 Charles Darwin's *The Origin of Species* forever changed the way we look at ourselves and our relationship to the cosmos. More recently, Ralph Nader's *Unsafe At Any Speed* and Rachel Carson's *Silent Spring* began movements for consumer safety and ecological consciousness. And in 1983 Howard Gardner changed the way we look at intelligence with *Frames of Mind*.

Written as a book for psychologists and pyschometricians, *Frames of Mind* has had an influence far greater than Gardner intended. More than pronouncements about the nature of intelligence, Gardner's theory of multiple intelligences (MI) has significantly affected educators and schools around the world. In *The Structure of the Scientific Revolution*, Thomas Kuhn coined the term "paradigm shift," which means looking at an established model or principle in a new way that forever changes its meaning. Gardner joins Stowe, Darwin, Nader, and Carson in writing a book that changed how we view a piece of the world.

2 | THE NEW CITY SCHOOL JOURNEY

At New City School, the theory of multiple intelligences (MI) is more than a theory of intellect. For us, it has become a philosophy of education with implications for the roles of educators, parents, and community members. MI has helped us frame our curriculum, develop new assessment techniques, work closely with our students' parents, and grow together as a faculty.

Perhaps the best way to capture what using MI has done for New City School is through the comment of a student. A few years ago, in response to being asked, "How do you like going to New City School?" one of our students said, "It's great but I can never tell when I'm learning and when I'm just having fun!" That response captures how MI can be a powerful tool for student growth. The student was expressing that he was able to use many of his intelligences in experiential, hands-on activities while he was learning.

In 1988 when I read *Frames of Mind* and we first began to pursue MI, none of us knew where this journey would lead. I would like to take credit for being prescient and a visionary and anticipating how working with MI would change our school, but that is not the case.

I knew that MI could be good for us, but I had no idea how we would be transformed.

Our journey to becoming an MI school was eased because the theory of multiple intelligences supported the faculty's tenets:

• All children have talents
• The arts are important
• Who you are is more important than what you know.

Pursuing MI seemed to make sense for us because it supports our beliefs and our deep commitment to valuing diversity in our student body. MI seemed to offer another way to recognize the uniqueness of each individual.

Beginning with a Reading Group

At one of our weekly faculty meetings in spring 1988 I told the staff about a fascinating book I had read, *Frames of Mind* (Gardner, 1983). I was particularly excited because I thought that it might have implications for our work with students. "Would any of you be interested in meeting after school and perhaps throughout the summer to read it with me?" I asked, offering to buy a copy of the book for everyone who wanted to join. A dozen individuals, about one-third of the faculty, chose to do so and we have not been the same since.

When we first met as a group, I began by offering a brief summary of the book. I talked about why it might have meaning for us, and how it caused me to reflect on what we were already doing to help all of our students grow as much as possible. Aside from investigating this theory of intelligences, I said, there would be merit in meeting and talking about the book, even if we ultimately believed the ideas were not applicable to New City School. "We are always sharing articles and trading books," I said. "This would simply take the pursuit to another level, a bigger group meeting more regularly."

Although we have subsequently read several books together, this was a new process for our faculty, so I offered some guidelines about how we might proceed. I envisioned a collaborative effort, each of us bringing something to the process and learning from one another. For added perspective, I suggested inviting a local university education department faculty member, who also happened to be a New City parent, to join us. Everyone was enthusiastic about her involvement.

I proposed that we all read the book and take turns presenting chapters to the group and facilitating the discussion. And I suggested preparing study questions that could be distributed before each meeting, showing my preference for the linguistic intelligence.

"But since we believe in team teaching," one of the teachers responded, "why don't we team-teach each chapter, working in groups of two?" This suggestion elicited lots of nods.

Another teacher said, "And if the idea is that children possess strengths in different intelligences and we are going to want to think about using them in our teaching, shouldn't we try to teach with the different intelligences?" Someone asked for clarification and she continued, "In presenting the chapter about the spatial intelligence, the teachers teaching it should try to rely on that intelligence, and the teachers teaching the chapter on the bodily-kinesthetic intelligence should use it in their instruction. That will give us an idea about whether or not this approach is realistic."

Using the different intelligences sounded like fun and we quickly embraced the idea. We decided to name ourselves the Talent Committee (feeling that calling ourselves the Intelligence Committee

might sound a bit presumptuous) and chose to meet every other week. A few meetings were held after school and then we met monthly during the summer, culminating our investigation the following winter.

Using the various intelligences as we studied them quickly transformed theory into real-life experience and opened the door to using MI in the classroom. I vividly remember stretching and straining as we played a modified game of Twister and then used our small-motor muscles as we tried to reassemble farming tools in learning about the bodily-kinesthetic intelligence. As we studied the chapter on musical intelligence, we played musical instruments, identified musical patterns, and tried to compose songs. We also talked with a professional musician, Jeremy Davenport, the son of our performing arts teacher. Jeremy plays the trumpet, has released several CDs, and has performed with Harry Connick Jr. Jeremy joined us during lunch one day to talk about how he learned through music and how irrelevant much of traditional schooling was for him.

An added, if painful, benefit of our investigation came as a result of trying to learn through all of the intelligences. We were reminded of what it feels like to perform poorly or even to fail. Most of us are successful because we have found roles that allow us to use our strongest intelligences; conversely, we generally are able to avoid participating in activities that require us to use our weakest intelligences. (Navigating like this, finding arenas in which we can use our strengths and where our weaknesses are less relevant, is evidence of strong intrapersonal intelligence.)

As members of the Talent Committee, each of us had to use all of our intelligences in studying the chapters in *Frames of Mind*. We did not have the option of steering away from our weakest intelligences. For example, music is not a strong intelligence of mine and I knew that, so I was neither surprised nor dismayed when I had difficulty participating in some of the committee's musical activities. But I had somehow assumed that my spatial intelligence was, if not a strength, at least not an area in which I was particularly weak. Much to my surprise, I found myself having great difficulty completing the mazes and discerning the patterns that were part of the activities for the spatial chapter. I realized what students must feel when they are forced to work in ways that require them to use the intelligences that are not their strongest. Because none of us can be strong in all of the intelligences, I was not alone in this experience. Other committee members also experienced frustration from using intelligences that they are typically able to avoid. Failing in front of our peers was a good, but hard, learning experience for all of us and a poignant reminder of how our students sometimes feel.

As we began to talk about the intelligences and how knowledge of them might be used to modify our curriculum and instruction, a teacher noted that we were already doing some things that supported MI. Instead of focusing only on what we were not doing, seeing the glass as half empty, we decided to create a list for each intelligence that captured the things we *were* doing. We also generated a list of things that we could and should be doing. And given our fiscal reality, we created a third category: things we could and should do that cost money. Our categories and ideas are shown in Figure 2.1.

Putting our thoughts in a simple table allowed us to celebrate the fine things we were already doing for our students, look consciously at how we might focus future efforts, and dream a bit about what we would like to do if we had the funds. The last category was particularly helpful because focusing on what we might do with additional funding, an unlikely prospect, also enabled us to focus more directly on what we might do without extra funds.

Getting Everyone On Board

After each of the first few meetings, the dialogue continued in conversations in the hall as people left to go to other commitments. They were excited about MI and its potential to help them reach their students. I was often in the teachers' lounge, talking about what we had said at a committee meeting, or in a casual conversation in the hall, discussing a point in the book. The dozen of us who were

Figure 2.1
Our Initial Thoughts About MI

Things we *already do* that support a belief in MI	Things we *could and should do* that support a belief in MI	Things we *could and should do* that support a belief in MI *that cost money*
1. Have an arts program that is an integral part of our curriculum 2. Focus on students learning to work with others	1. Use student portfolios to show work in all intelligences 2. Begin report cards by addressing what is most important: the personal intelligences	1. Have a video camera in each classroom to capture students exhibiting nonpaper-and-pencil intelligences 2. Bring in practicing visual and performing artists to work with our students

engaged in this journey were brimming with enthusiasm and ideas.

Near the end of the next Talent Committee meeting, however, a teacher voiced a concern. "I'm worried that there is beginning to be a rift between those of us who are on the Talent Committee and those who aren't." Our group grew quiet as she continued, "One of my teammates asked me, 'What is all of this business about intelligences?'"

Most of us who have worked in schools have seen the phenomenon of the "in" group or popular crowd. It doesn't matter why a group is perceived as the "in" group. It may be that the reasons are worthy; for example, a group of teachers is very skilled, works hard, or is open to innovation and trying new things. Or it may simply be that a particular group of teachers is perceived to be in the principal's favor. Frankly, why a group is perceived to be "in" isn't important. What is important is that, if one group is "in," everyone else must be "out." And, a divided faculty cannot move forward together.

The teacher's observation resonated with us. We knew that we wanted to avoid having a divided faculty as we continued studying *Frames of Mind* and worked on using what we learned. As we talked, everyone expressed a concern that our work not become an issue that divided the faculty. But what to do? We had just begun our investigation, but it was already obvious that everyone wouldn't be serving on the committee. Some teachers wanted to participate in the discussion of the Talent Committee, but did not have the time or weren't available at the scheduled meeting times. Others were more skeptical about the existence of multiple intelligences and chose not to participate on the committee. Still others were newer to the teaching profession and were focusing on basic teaching strategies and classroom control. Clearly, not everyone would be on the Talent Committee, so not everyone would be privy to new information and

discussions. We knew that we needed to solve the problem.

As we talked, we devised a conscious strategy to avoid having divisions among the faculty. First, I made it clear that membership on the Talent Committee was always open and anyone could elect to join at any time. Although no new members joined until the fall, the option made the group seem less exclusive. Second, at each weekly faculty meeting and in my periodic faculty bulletins, references were made to what the Talent Committee had learned and discussed. All the committee members tried to share not just specific information but also our enthusiasm for the potential that we saw in MI. At one meeting we made a point of assigning Talent Committee members to talk with their teammates about specific ideas and activities—for example, the possibility of using portfolios to show student growth.

Throughout the initial MI investigation, and even today, having everyone on board is an important consideration. For example, during the winter after our implementation of MI, ASCD held an MI Conference at the Key School in Indianapolis (the first MI school). The Talent Committee talked about how this conference was an opportunity to widen the net and bring more folks into the MI fold. As a result, we sent eight faculty members to the conference, sending four who were on the Talent Committee and four who were not. We even decided to travel in two cars and be sure that each car had only two people from the Talent Committee. In retrospect, this arrangement may seem overly structured and contrived; in fact, however, throughout our MI journey we never experienced division among faculty members. Although our faculty's openness to new ideas and an established culture of collaboration were no doubt important to our success, our conscious efforts to be as inclusive as possible during our investigation were critical to maintaining a positive and collegial workplace.

How MI Has Affected Us

Today, more than a decade after we read *Frames of Mind*, our use of MI has transformed our school. It has affected curriculum and instruction, assessment practices, relationships with our students' parents, and collegiality.

Curriculum and Instruction

Using MI means that students are given opportunities to use intelligences other than the linguistic and logical-mathematical intelligences in their regular classrooms. Too often the "nonscholastic intelligences," if addressed at all, are the sole province of the art or physical education teachers. We respect the expertise of these individuals and do not want to supplant their efforts, but we try to enable students to use their strongest intelligences in learning traditional subject matter and skills. This means that students sometimes draw Venn diagrams to identify and explain relationships among groups, using their logical-mathematical intelligence to show, for example, the similarities and differences between those who dumped tea at the Boston Tea Party and those who marched in the Civil Rights struggle. Or they create T-shirt book reports, using the spatial intelligence to report on what they read. Or students might use their bodily-kinesthetic intelligence to jump rope and count aloud to learn addition.

Almost no lesson includes entry points for all eight intelligences; that would be neither realistic nor practical. Students are given choices, however; for instance, they can draw a picture or create a dance or compose a song to show their understanding of a poem—all alternatives to the usual approach of expressing understanding through the linguistic intelligence. In every area, students regularly review their work, reflecting on their efforts, noting the mistakes they made, and making suggestions about how they could improve. They adopt trees, making periodic drawings and journal entries to monitor their growth and change through the seasons. Students may create museums to show what they know—museums about plants or snakes, museums in which students dress up as the famous people they have studied. MI fits especially well with our creative approach to curriculum development. Although we have specific grade-level expectations, teachers develop their own curriculum units to achieve their goals; the few textbooks are used as supplements.

Amidst the creativity of MI applications there is a place for mastery of rote facts, reading, writing, and basic computation. While we value all of the intelligences, we recognize that our students must be skilled in reading, writing, and mathematics. Using MI gives us more tools to help students learn and to make learning interesting. What MI means, most of all, is that students are viewed as individuals. Rather than molding students to an established curriculum, creating winners and losers, an MI approach means developing curriculum and using instruction that taps into students' interests and talents. Students are given options, different ways to learn, and they share responsibility for their learning.

We began to use yearlong schoolwide themes at the same time that we started using MI. We felt that thematic instruction would offer continuity and make learning more meaningful, nicely supporting our efforts to integrate MI into curriculum and instruction. Our first theme, Life Along the River, was enjoyed by everyone. The synergy of siblings in different grades at New City School talking at dinner or on the way to school about what they had learned about the Mississippi River in their respective classes was great, and so was the dialogue among teachers from different grades as they were trading ideas and talking about how they were bringing the river into their classroom. By Thanksgiving, however, we realized that even if each year's focus on the river was different and developmentally appropriate as our students moved from grade to grade, they would feel that they were learning the same thing each year.

To avoid the feeling of repetition, we knew our idea of themes would have to be revisited. Although we were just a few months into using themes, we had already felt the positive effects, such as how themes could help us organize our curriculum and focus our efforts. Because we didn't want to abandon the idea, we decided that each grade's team of teachers would develop their own yearlong theme; we continue doing so today. The

themes stem from teachers' passions and interests, each being a vehicle to address schoolwide expectations and goals. Teachers refine and build upon their themes from year to year. Sample grade-level themes for a school year and sample focus questions are shown in Figure 2.2.

Assessment Practices

Using MI in curriculum and instruction means that students learn and show their understanding in many different ways. While paper and pencil measures—essays and objective tests—have their role,

FIGURE 2.2
Sample Grade Level Themes

Grade and Theme	Sample Focus
3- and 4-year-old class: All About Me	Who am I and how do I fit within my family and class?
4- and 5-year-old class: We Are All Alike, We Are All Different	How are people, their families, and communities alike and different?
Kindergarten: Busy Bodies	How do the different systems in my body function?
1st grade: It's a Small World	How do plant and animal communities compare with human communities?
2nd grade: All Kinds of Homes	Why and how do people make homes different in their communities?
3rd grade: Native Americans, Keepers of the Earth	How did Native Americans live from and with the land?
4th grade: Making a Difference	What are the characteristics of someone who makes a difference?
5th grade: Conflict	How are conflicts caused by different views over needs, values, and resources?
6th grade: Understanding the World from Within and Without	What is the role of choice in determining who we are?

they invariably limit the students' responses to a few intelligences. If the question is "How much do 3rd graders know about life for a Native American tribe in the 1850s?" then a written response is not the only way to determine a student's understanding. Yes, a student essay allows the teacher to ascertain what the student knows, but it is not the only way to do so. By limiting students to writing their answers, relying on their linguistic skills, the teacher may find out whether a student has a good command of the English language and writes well, but she may shortchange students' understanding of Native American culture and history in other ways.

In addition to simply writing about Native American life, why not have the student use a Venn diagram to show how a Navajo tribe in 1850 lives similarly to and differently from a family in Chicago today? Or how about having the student, or teams of students, create a diorama of Navajo life? Or can a student put words to a melody and convey what life was like for the Navajo? Can the student draw a picture that portrays an understanding of the Navajo culture? The students would still need to explain the thinking behind their actions, but in each case student understanding would not have to be filtered through only a linguistic lens.

Each spring our first floor hall becomes a walkway to America's past as each of our 40 3rd graders creates and displays a diorama depicting the life of a Native American tribe. Similarly, our 4th graders demonstrate their knowledge at a "state fair" in which they choose one state from the United States and create a three-dimensional display. Our graduating 6th graders' culminating experience is an autobiography that results in a detailed book including narrative, survey results, drawings, photos, and reflections.

Many of our classes plan and create museums of artifacts and displays to demonstrate their knowledge and educate others. The 1st graders'

plant museum displays plants and results of student-conducted experiments for visitors to see. To learn about museums, the class divides into groups and visits local museums; they apply their observations in planning their own exhibits. New City's 4th graders present a living museum in which they dress in costume to portray the individuals who made a difference in an area of the curriculum they have studied. As visitors press start buttons taped to the student statues, the statues spring to life and begin to tell their stories.

Projects, exhibitions, presentations, and portfolios are used a great deal by students to show what they have learned. By working together on projects, students are also developing personal intelligences while they learn content and skill. Portfolios are cumulative, kept from year to year, and reviewed each spring with parents at a Portfolio Night. (See Chapter 4 for more on assessment.)

Relationships with Students' Parents

Because we use MI, we communicate with our students' parents. We recognize that New City is very different from the schools they attended, and that we have a responsibility to help them understand what we are doing. I send parents a weekly note, as do the classroom teachers. These letters announce upcoming events and happenings but also discuss the curriculum and what children are learning. We also communicate with parents by displaying student work and descriptions of the assignments in our halls and on our classroom walls.

Perhaps our most powerful tool for developing positive and richer relations with students' parents is our September Intake Conference. Everyone knows that at this conference the parents, who are experts on their children, are expected to talk 75 percent of the time and teachers are expected to listen 75 percent of the time. Beginning the year with parents talking and teachers listening is a wonderful way to learn about students, and it sets a tone that says to parents, "We are all working together to help your children—our students—learn."

Faculty Collegiality

Implementing MI, moving forward in uncharted waters, meant that we had to work and learn together. None of us had *the* solution. MI helped us recognize that all of us have different intelligence profiles; not only do we learn differently, we teach differently too. Teaching teams became more than people working together and supplying emotional support; using MI meant that teams began to draw upon the expertise and interests of each member in planning curriculum and instruction. For example, a team uses strengths when one teacher plays the piano and brings music into units and lessons. Another teacher's spatial talents are used to create the signs and backdrops for student projects. The third teacher's logical-mathematical strength helps her identify patterns in instruction and relate activities to one another. In other teams, students might rotate among the teachers as they use their strongest intelligence to teach a lesson.

Perhaps the best evidence of our collegiality is the two books of articles and lesson plans written by our faculty, *Celebrating Multiple Intelligences: Teaching for Success* (1994) and *Succeeding with Multiple Intelligences: Teaching Through the Personals* (1996).* Before writing the articles and contributing the lesson plans, faculty members had to agree on what the book should look like and how it should be structured. These kinds of conversations, caused and supported by our work with MI, have helped us grow and learn together. As proud as I am of our faculty's books, I know that the dialogue that took place in creating them is far more important. Not every faculty will choose to produce books, but using MI can facilitate faculty members trading curriculum and instruction ideas and sharing their skills in the intelligences.

A Work in Progress

All of our achievements and progress notwithstanding, we still have far to go to be the kind of school that we want to be. We continue to grapple with the incredible demands of time and energy that are brought on by our creating and developing curriculum and assessment tools and by our own never-decreasing expectations! When asked to name the best thing about teaching at New City School, a teacher once replied, "That's easy. I get to create my own curriculum, decide how my students are going to be assessed, and work with others who are creative and energetic." And what is the *worst* thing about teaching at New City? "That's easy, too," she said. "I get to create my own curriculum, decide how my students are going to be assessed, and work with others who are creative and energetic."

✦ ✦ ✦

For Faculty Discussion

1. Which intelligences are valued most in our school?
2. What are the obstacles to implementing MI in our school?
3. In which intelligence is our faculty the strongest? Weakest?
4. How would our school's ideas fit into Figure 2.1?

Steps to Implementing MI

Each school and each MI journey is different. The following tips, however, may be helpful in any pursuit of MI.

1. Educate *all* the stakeholders. While it is essential to begin by building consensus within the faculty—reading and discussing a book on MI is a

---

*For more information about these books, contact the New City School.

good way to begin—it is crucial that parents and community members also understand how what we are doing works for students.

• Use the halls and walls to educate everyone about MI, not just display student work.

• Write parents weekly notes that educate them about MI and the many ways in which it is helping their children grow.

• Give standardized tests to reassure everyone that students are learning the basic competencies they need to succeed in school.

2. Measure what you value. Unless assessment practices and reporting techniques reflect MI, the message is that the nonscholastic intelligences really aren't important.

• Construct report cards that emphasize and value all the intelligences.

• Invite parents to hear and see their children exhibit learning through their presentations and projects.

• Use portfolios as powerful tools for capturing growth in the nonscholastic intelligences.

3. Intentionally develop collegiality. A school is no better than its faculty, and pursuing MI can be effective only if teachers and administrators learn and grow with one another. There is already more to be done than the hours allow, so unless collegiality is a priority, unless specific strategies are developed to facilitate faculty members sharing, it will not happen.

• Form a voluntary faculty reading group.

• Make faculty members aware of the notion of collegiality and its value. Ask "How can we work toward this?"

• Use faculty meetings to share teaching strategies and professional achievements.

3 | COLLEGIALITY: LEARNING AND GROWING TOGETHER

Barth (1990) believes that the most important factor in determining the quality of a school is the nature of the adult relationships within that school. Productive relationships involve more than working congenially with others in the building. Although all of us want to get along with others, we need to strive for more than just a pleasant working environment; we need to strive for *collegiality*. Collegiality means educators working with and learning from one another as colleagues, as partners.

As powerful as the theory of multiple intelligences can be in changing how educators view students, a school is not likely to succeed at using MI productively without a high degree of collegiality. I can conceive of good schools in which the educators do not subscribe to MI theory; I cannot imagine a good school in which the staff do not work together as colleagues. In an MI school, collegiality is especially important because educators create curriculum, design instructional strategies, and invent assessments tools. Teachers and administrators work as colleagues to fashion strategies that reflect their assumptions and respect the unique contexts in which they work. Unfortunately, schools typically have focused too little on teachers' and administrators' learning, and it is a rare school that encourages teachers and administrators to learn from one another.

Why Is Collegiality Difficult?

Collegiality does not come easily in a school environment for four primary reasons:

1. Students are the focus of our efforts. It's difficult for educators to rationalize spending money on a book written for teachers when students are using outdated textbooks. Attending a workshop or traveling to a conference is too often a rare occurrence in an era of budget-cutting and austerity.

2. New, and therefore unproven, educational trends and directions are viewed as suspect and risky. It is politically safer to remain with old traditions and activities. Educators are more likely to be criticized for trying something new and not succeeding than for continuing along the road of the tried and true, even though the existing strategy has not been successful. By staying the course, they continue to work in relative isolation, because they have little need to work with or learn from others.

3. Most schools are not designed for collaboration or collegiality. Classrooms are enclosed spaces with rows of student desks and one teacher's desk. Seldom is there a space designed for teachers to work together and exchange ideas, such as a conference room with comfortable chairs, a large table, dry-erase boards, and computers—a customary set-up for the average business. In contrast, the gathering place for teachers is the lounge, typically a crowded place to eat and relax, filled with

secondhand furniture. Architects and planners have not seen the need to provide an environment that supports the faculty learning as colleagues.

4. Finally, and perhaps most important, schools are not organized to support collegiality. In *Redesigning School*, Joseph P. McDonald (1996) points out that for teachers, "there is literally no time built in for learning on the job. Indeed, learning on the job is disparaged to some extent" (p. 105). Working together is often defined as teachers sharing materials. The reward system of schools neither encourages nor reinforces teachers who take the time to lend a hand and share their expertise. At best, educators have come to feel that their good ideas shouldn't be shared because they might appear to be bragging. At worst, good ideas are hoarded because a teacher wants to ensure that what students experience in her room is unique. Principals are too busy with paperwork, disciplinary matters, and staff supervision to work at creating a climate in which the adults work collegially.

All these factors conspire to create a setting where adult learning takes place in isolation. And yet, we have learned that many students learn best when they work with others. Along with individual mastery, cooperative learning has an important role in student learning and achievement. Why should learning be any different for adults?

Collegiality as a Route to MI

As noted earlier, MI theory is not a curriculum. Consequently, there is an opportunity for each teacher—preferably for each group of teachers—to use MI in ways that respect their unique setting. Because this means traveling in uncharted educational waters, the pursuit of MI can encourage faculty to work together as colleagues on a journey of understanding. Indeed, a successful implementation of MI means that the school becomes, in Peter Senge's (1990) terminology, "a learning organization."

Roland Barth (1990) offers four ways in which educators can work as colleagues: (1) teachers and administrators talking together about students' growth and students' needs, (2) teachers and administrators working together to develop curriculum, (3) teachers and administrators observing one another teach, and (4) teachers and administrators teaching one another. To Barth's components, I add: Teachers and administrators working together on faculty committees to reflect on current practices and plan for the future. And, more important than any of these specific tactics is the underlying premise that by working together, we can achieve more than by working in isolation.

While MI implementations vary, the following represent some examples of how collegiality and MI implementation go hand-in-hand.

Student Growth and Needs

Believing in and using MI means that educators must be aware of students' strengths and weaknesses in the various intelligences; in short, educators must know their students. MI becomes a tool to help students learn information and skills and to enable them to demonstrate their understanding. To use MI effectively, teachers need to know each student's strongest and weakest intelligences. Knowing each student, teachers can design curriculum and present instruction in ways that allow students to use their strengths, although few lessons will offer eight routes to learning.

To learn about their students, teachers need structured time to share information and to learn from one another's perceptions. Teachers sometimes share information about their students with other teachers, but they rarely discuss those who are achieving, or as Gardner calls them, "at-promise" students. Working together as colleagues, faculty members can share perceptions about how they view students when they are using different intelligences. Sitting around a table, comparing notes on their students, teachers might say

- "Paul's collection of butterflies and insects was incredible. I've never seen him so analytical!"

- "Why do you think René seems so much more motivated in English than in social studies?"

- "Brad excels when he can use his spatial intelligence to show me what he knows!"

- "It was amazing to see Samantha go through her portfolio and talk about how she learns."

- "Mei-Lee filters everything through her musical intelligence."

- "Lee's interpersonal intelligence is so strong, I always try to have her work in a group."

- "I wasn't sure Langston understood the Navajo life style until he began to explain his diorama to me."

- "It's interesting, I have seen that Carl is so motivated at recess or in P.E. class when he is using his bodily-kinesthetic intelligence. I need to find a way to let him capitalize on this strength in learning about the Civil War."

MI becomes another way to individualize instruction, another way to look at how Jacqueline is different from José who is different from Juanita who is different from John. Viewing and talking about students from the perspective of MI enables us to look at how each student is unique. We need to know how students learn best in order to adjust our curriculum and instruction. Some teachers teach a subject or discipline that lends itself to a particular intelligence, such as English or physical education. It is important for these teachers to hear how teachers in other subject areas or academic disciplines, especially those that rely on other intelligences, see their students. Talking about students from the viewpoint of multiple intelligences is a good way to focus on how they learn best. Each teacher has a different perspective, and by sharing their observations teachers can more quickly get to know their students' strengths. Specialist teachers who encounter each student for only a portion of the day especially benefit from these shared observations.

Similarly, teachers in self-contained classrooms can observe how their students respond to different subjects and instruction. If John struggles with reading but is incredibly motivated when drawing, how can his strength in the spatial intelligence be used to address the prescribed curriculum goals and help him learn? The answer is more likely to be found if teachers share their perceptions of John and their strategies for teaching him.

Recording how students solve problems offers valuable insights. Sometimes the easiest way to identify students' strongest intelligences is to give them choices and observe what they select. Most students, indeed most people, choose the route that allows them to use their most developed intelligences.

Faculty Jointly Develops Curriculum

Students learn best and teachers teach best when teachers develop, modify, and personalize the curriculum. Yet in most cases state and district expectations and publisher's scope and sequence paths need to be followed. Textbooks often serve as default curriculum guides, becoming the teacher's planner. Regardless, teachers have opportunities to work collaboratively to decide the best ways to accomplish goals and expectations. Whether it is planning lessons, developing units, or deciding upon yearlong themes, teachers and administrators can create both the experiences in which children can learn and the methods by which to determine what learning has taken place. Using the MI framework helps plan an array of experiences and activities that allow all children, not just the linguistically or logical-mathematically inclined, to use their strongest intelligences in learning.

Teachers naturally teach using their strongest intelligences. The linguistically intelligent teacher explains everything; lectures are his modus operandi even when teaching about history or art. No matter what the subject, the teacher who is strongest in the logical-mathematical intelligence looks for formulas and rules when teaching. Although I may have exaggerated these descriptions, they have more than a few kernels of truth. Because schools are framed around these two scholastic intelligences and because people who choose to become teachers tend to be those who did well in school, it is only natural that most teachers rely on the linguistic and logical-mathematical intelligences. Students strongest in the scholastic intelligences benefit from these approaches, but what about students with strengths in the other intelligences? They probably can gain the most from teachers and administrators working together to make learning more accessible for all students. Here are some examples of teachers working together to figure out ways to incorporate MI into their instruction:

"This is the time of year when I introduce *The Popcorn Book* to my students," says a 1st grade teacher, "but I want to do more than just read it aloud and appeal only to the linguistic intelligence. Any ideas?"

A 5th grade math teacher responds, "Why don't you actually pop popcorn, not just to eat, but to get the kids hypothesizing and estimating, using their logical-mathematical intelligences? You could have the kids guess where the kernels would land, pop it without the lid on, and then measure where the kernels landed, graphing the predicted versus actual distance."

The music teacher adds, "What about making rhythm instruments from the cardboard tube inside paper towels? You could fill them with kernels of corn and enclose the ends."

The 1st grade teacher interrupts, "And while having the kids use them as rhythm instruments is good, I could also have them use the shakers to identify the number of syllables in words. We're working on that now!"

Two other teachers brainstorm about ways that the 3rd grade teachers can use both the logical-

mathematical and spatial intelligences in helping their students appreciate the enormous size of the buffalo. They decide to use masking tape to create the silhouette of a full-size buffalo on the classroom floor and have kids invent units of measure using parts of their bodies to calculate how big it is. "This way I can address both measurement and proportion, two of my math goals, in my Native American unit," says the 3rd grade teacher.

Another 3rd grade teacher talks about using the outdoors, tapping into students' naturalist intelligence, to encourage writing. "Some of my kids who have difficulty creating rich descriptions were completely different when we were looking at how the leaves change colors in the fall," she said. "As a result, we each adopted a nearby tree and periodically go outside to make observations and record them in our journals."

At the other end of the table a 4th grade teacher is discussing his frustration with a unit on biographies. "I know they're important," he laments, "because our students need to understand the genre of biography and how it's different from autobiography, fiction, and so on. And I appreciate the value of studying famous people whose character and virtues made them successful, but for those kids who are having difficulty reading and writing, producing these biographies becomes a real ordeal and they get turned off from learning."

"Why not adapt what we did last year in our unit about snakes?" responds a 2nd grade teacher. "So many of our kids, especially those few who were not yet reading, excelled when they gave oral presentations to their classmates and parents. You could have your kids dress up like the characters they're studying and create a living museum, in which they would pose as statues until visitors press their button. At that prompt, the kids spring to life and tell 'their' life stories, the biographies!"

The music teacher adds, "That would be great for Carlton. You've told me he is not a good reader, but he comes alive in my class when he is performing in front of others!"

A 6th grade teacher asks others how they develop reflection sheets, as she looks for ways to capture her students' intrapersonal intelligence in their biographies. And 5th grade teachers talk about using Venn diagrams to determine how well their students understand the similarities and differences between the Civil War and the Civil Rights Movement.

All of these examples are taken from the New City School. These practices worked for our kids and they came from teachers and administrators talking together about how MI can be used to modify curriculum so that every child can learn.

Observation Opportunities

The norms of education do not support educators observing one another teach, certainly not teachers observing peers teach. The presence of an adult, other than the teacher, in the classroom often means there is a problem. An administrator may formally observe a teacher during class, but the observation is often focused on determining whether a teacher's contract should be renewed, not on growth. Teachers typically visit other classrooms only to borrow something, to ask a question, or to briefly check on an activity. Sara Lawrence Lightfoot, author of *The Good High School*, says, "Teaching is a very autonomous experience—but the flip side of autonomy is that teachers experience loneliness and isolation" (in Moyers, 1989, p. 165).

As teachers, we spend most of our days with youngsters. And while students invariably offer us feedback on how well they think we teach—whether we want it or not!—they cannot give us targeted feedback to enable us become better teachers. Students cannot help us reflect on wait-time or on our success with problem-based learning, constructivism, or action research.

When pursuing MI, however, a faculty has the opportunity to change the paradigm. Because we all have a unique MI profile, we recognize that others approach curriculum and instruction differently. Thus it becomes obvious that we can learn from others whether or not they teach the same discipline or age level. Teachers can feel comfortable using their strongest intelligences in sharing with peers, both while teaching peers and being observed. Spatially talented teachers, for example, can demonstrate how they incorporate this intelligence in teaching Shakespeare, and how they enable students to use it in demonstrating their understanding of the historical period and culture in which the *Taming Of the Shrew* was written (perhaps through designing a city map or travel poster of London during that time). While our profession's norms can make it difficult or awkward for one teacher to share with another teacher her strategy for teaching two-digit division, describing how she uses her musical intelligence to teach equivalent fractions is easy—and welcomed by nonmusical colleagues. We easily accept that we are not strong in every intelligence and readily look to others who have strengths different from our own.

Extensive work with MI sometimes leads teachers to conclude that they should capitalize on their strengths and interests by having students rotate among a set of teachers, each teacher focusing on the same concepts through different intelligences. Teacher-taught centers that address the various intelligences can be created and shared. Or classes can come together to watch one teacher display a skill or understanding in an intelligence. In a unit on government, for example, our 4th grade teachers invited the band teacher to come to their classes and instruct students on how to create a melody and set their poetry to music.

It is helpful to develop guidelines for teachers to use in observing each other, rather than encouraging open-ended observation and discussion. For example, the observing teacher might enter the classroom with three goals: (1) to identify three things that she'd like to try, (2) to find something positive to share with the teacher being observed, and (3) to find one thing to ask questions about. A structured situation is far less threatening to both teachers.

Reciprocal Teaching

Again, because MI is not a set curriculum, teachers and administrators have the opportunity to learn together by teaching one another. When members of our faculty read *Frames of Mind*, we did it as a voluntary committee. Pairs of faculty members took responsibility for presenting a chapter to the rest of the group, teaching with the particular intelligence described in that chapter. Likewise, as we embarked on using portfolios to help us capture students' progress, different teachers took the lead in helping us read and discuss articles. Today, we are pursuing genuine understanding—students using skills and knowledge in new and novel situations—as colleagues teaching one another and learning together. It is clear that none of us is the expert, that we all have experiences, ideas, and talents to bring to the table. Learning from one another becomes a necessity.

Faculty book groups have played an important role in our teaching one another. Participation in these groups is optional, but they are great opportunities for administrators and teachers to work together. Meeting every couple of weeks, either before school or during the summer, members of our faculty have read books chosen because they supported our mission. Looking at how to meet student needs, we have read *Frames of Mind* (Gardner, 1983), *The Unschooled Mind* (Gardner, 1991), *Improving Schools from Within* (Barth, 1990), *Emotional Intelligence* (Goleman, 1995), and *The Teaching for Understanding Guide* (Blythe, 1998). With diversity as our focus, we read *Warriors Don't Cry* (Beals, 1994),

Daughters (Early, 1994), *I Know Why the Caged Bird Sings* (Angelou, 1970), and *White Teacher* (Paley, 1979). Our discussions invariably range from reactions to the books to explanations of our personal educational philosophies to recollections of specific instances in the classroom. More than simply sharing ideas and opinions, participants gain a sense of respect and trust for one another.

Reflecting and Planning

We view faculty committees as the primary engine for driving collegiality. Schoolwide committees, by their very nature, focus on long-term, transcendent issues. We expect that each teacher will serve on at least one faculty committee, and many choose to participate in several committees. Cross-grade committees place teachers next to and alongside other teachers and faculty with whom they might not normally work.

We typically have four or five committees during a school year, each meeting every two or three weeks. We always have a Diversity Committee, whose charge is to increase awareness of racial and socioeconomic diversity issues among our faculty, as well as to develop curriculum. We usually have a committee that deals with implementing MI (the Talent Committee), a Portfolio Committee, and at least one other ad hoc committee. One year, for example, we had a Parent Communication Committee, which designed our Progress Reports (report cards) and came up with the idea for our September Intake Conferences. In previous years we have had an Assembly Committee, a Technology Committee, an Assessment Committee, and a committee on schoolwide behavior expectations and standards. Administrators and teachers work as partners, collegially, on committees.

Collegiality is more an attitude than a strategy. If MI is to be successfully implemented schoolwide, however, collegiality must be present. Administrators have an opportunity to promote collegiality by acknowledging it in teachers' end-of-year evaluations and praising teachers who model this quality. If we measure what we value, then we need to show that we truly value teachers working as colleagues. More important, administrators can model it by working collegially with their administrative team and by learning with and from their faculty members.

◆ ◆ ◆

For Faculty Discussion

1. What evidence is there that collegiality is valued in our school?
2. As we proceed along the path of learning and collegiality, what can we do to ensure that we don't wind up with an "in group" and an "out group"?
3. How could we encourage and support teachers from different grades or disciplines working together on curriculum?

Steps to Implementing MI

Each school and each MI journey is different. The following tips, however, may be helpful in any pursuit of MI.

1. Is there interest in a before- or after-school faculty book club? Even if "only" four or five faculty members participate, it is a good use of time for them (and a good beginning for everyone).
2. Set aside some time at faculty meetings for teachers to share successful strategies. If it is difficult to begin, ask teachers to submit questions on 3" x 5" cards to get the dialogue started.
3. Combining congeniality and collegiality, offer before- or after-school classes one day each week in art, music, or some aspect of physical education for teachers and faculty. These classes help the adults in the school community begin to learn and work with colleagues while developing their own intelligences. (A bonus is the visibility the classes offer to the various intelligences and the specialist teachers who teach them.)

4 | Assessing and Reporting Student Growth

The relationship between curriculum, instruction, and assessment needs to be strong. That we give more time and attention to teaching skills and behaviors on which students will be evaluated is only appropriate. But *how* we assess also plays a role in determining what and how we teach. Assessing students in ways that draw upon only linguistic and logical-mathematical intelligences is both an injustice to students and a failure to help parents view their children with a wider lens. A commitment to MI should not only affect how we design curriculum and present instruction, but also how we assess student progress.

Good assessment is relevant, ongoing, and authentic; students learn from their performances on meaningful tasks. Students need to be able to read, write, and compute well, so there is a place for them to use their linguistic and logical-mathematical skills (their scholastic intelligences) in showing what they know. Sometimes performances of understanding need to be displayed in a particular intelligence, such as using the linguistic intelligence to show mastery of essay writing or using the logical-mathematical intelligence to demonstrate whether it is better to purchase or lease an automobile.

In good instruction, the line between curriculum and assessment becomes fuzzy. Assessment is not only a culminating, end-of-unit activity. Instead, students show what they know by monitoring themselves and learning from their performance as they progress. Consequently, we need summative assessments of finished products, assessments that show what students know and can do, as well as cumulative assessments, assessments that show *how* a problem was solved and the points of progress along the learning route. Each of these kinds of assessment provides insights into student thinking and also provides the student with information about personal achievement. And as the various intelligences are woven into instruction, they should be included in assessment.

We need to be careful, however, to use "intelligence-fair" assessments (Krechevsky, Hoerr, and Gardner, 1994) whenever possible to enable students to use their stronger intelligences to show what they know rather than forcing them to use a linguistic filter to demonstrate their understanding. If the goal is comparing and contrasting the Lincoln and Kennedy presidencies, for example, why not allow students to do this by making a Venn diagram or poster rather than requiring them to write about it? Why not allow students to create a skit or role play to illustrate the law of supply and demand? If we want to know whether students understand a certain principle in physics, we should ask them to build a pulley and lever system and demonstrate it rather than having them respond to multiple-choice items. Why not allow students to show that they understand a poem by creating a song or dance?

Reporting Assessment to Various Audiences

Educators decry parents who focus on grades and standardized test scores, yet we often share only these measures of student progress. We need to recognize that there are many different assessment audiences and that not only *what* we assess, but also *why* and *how* we assess vary with the audience:

• For students, assessments provide feedback on their performance and enable them to increase their intrapersonal intelligence. Students can use all intelligences in learning and showing what they have learned.

• For students' parents, assessments provide information on how their children are progressing. Appropriate assessments can give parents confidence in a school that is quite different from the schools they attended. Although parents can see their children's growth in all intelligences, educating parents about MI (e.g., through assessment) allows them to better appreciate the value of the intelligences.

• For educators, assessments help us know what a student has mastered and what still needs more attention. Assessments also enable us to gain feedback about the job we are doing. In particular, it is interesting to see how students' performance changes as they are given opportunities to use all of their intelligences.

• For the larger community, assessments generate confidence that students are prepared to succeed in society. Unless the community is educated and sees the value of the nonscholastic intelligences, the larger community will resort to focusing almost exclusively on standardized test data. It is the responsibility of the educators to help community members see that there are other, richer ways of measuring student progress. Inviting community

members to visit the school and observe student presentations can be an effective way to educate the public.

• For the larger educational institution (the school or district's board of education, state board, and department of education), assessments indicate that we are fulfilling our responsibilities and ensure confidence in students' learning and preparation for higher learning. Given the press for objectivity and vast numbers of students applying for limited slots, these groups rely on standardized test data, which primarily measure the scholastic intelligences.

Most educational institutions rely on standardized test scores, which show success in the scholastic intelligences, to ascertain quality of student preparation. These data can be valuable, but they capture only a portion of student talents and achievements. Although policymakers and governmental entities rely on standardized test data, those who truly want to know students' strengths and weaknesses—including the students—can learn much when viewing progress in the nonscholastic intelligences. Communicating about student progress in the spatial, bodily-kinesthetic, musical, naturalist, intrapersonal, or interpersonal intelligences also offers an opportunity to educate parents and others about MI theory and how it can help children learn. We can capture student growth through all of the intelligences in several ways that will allow us to satisfy the assessment needs of the various audiences.

Projects, Exhibitions, and Presentations (PEPs)

Asking children to show their understanding by creating projects, exhibitions, and presentations (PEPs) opens up a world of possibilities. Because PEPs are all complex acts, they require (as do all complex acts) students to use several intelligences. Using PEPs means that students not only have to be knowledgeable about their topics, it also means that they have to use their personal intelligences. Beyond learning the content or skill, students need to think about the best way to present the information to their audiences. In making presentations, students work on making eye contact, enunciating and pacing their speech, projecting their voices, and "reading" their audiences. PEPs are often done as collaborative activities with two or more students using their interpersonal intelligences to work together as a team. Students reflect on their performance, sometimes reviewing videotapes of a previous effort in their planning.

Fourth graders at New City School culminate their unit on the states, for example, by selecting a state, studying it, and preparing a report that they present to other students and adults. The 4th graders use all of their intelligences in displaying their understanding. Reports are presented in a three-dimensional format, each including a student-created game for visitors to play in testing their knowledge about the states.

The 6th graders prepare narrative autobiographies that also include photos, drawings, bar and line graphs, survey results, and songs that the students feel capture who they are. The autobiographies are presented to family members, friends, and other students.

Report Cards and Progress Reports

Report cards, or progress reports, are formal communications about student progress. They are not just read and discarded, but are often shared with other family members and coworkers. Sometimes report cards are tucked in a drawer and referred to years later. They carry a weight and symbolism that cannot be ignored; more to the point, they offer an opportunity to educate as well as report. By what the report cards focus upon and by what they ignore, we send messages to students and parents about what is important. Each faculty should look

at a blank copy of the school's report card and ask, "Are we showing what we value by what we are reporting in the report cards?"

At New City, we believe that the personal intelligences are the most important intelligences. Consequently, we designed our progress reports so that the entire first page addresses the personal intelligences and is accompanied by a personalized narrative report. The next two pages contain rubrics for both the linguistic and logical-mathematical intelligences and also include narrative reports about the student's progress. Personalized narrative reports offer context (describing what the class has worked on during this reporting period) and a way to document the student's efforts in demonstrating knowledge through PEPs. Figure 4.1 (pp. 28–29) shows a sample of the logical-mathematical page and narrative comments.

The progress report also includes specialists' reports for the musical, spatial, and bodily-kinesthetic intelligences, as well as reports from the science, library, and Spanish teachers, each on a separate page. Appendix B shows the full text of our progress reports. These reports are sent home twice each year. Used with our other reporting techniques and measures, the progress report shares information about a child's strengths and the areas where the student is weak. Note, too, how the reports educate parents about our curriculum.

Our teachers devote considerable skill and time to preparing these reports. They are an investment in the future of our school. The effort that goes into the preparation (talking with teammates ahead of time to share perceptions of student progress) and writing not only ensures that parents will have a rich understanding of their child's growth, it also helps educate parents about MI and our program. By using the MI vocabulary and focusing on the personal intelligences in each of our specialist's reports, we help parents see how their children's different intelligences are used in school. The reports are sent home before conferences so that parents have time to review them before meeting with teachers. Parents treasure the reports, often commenting that they appreciate the work of the teachers and how well their children are understood.

The progress reports, sent home twice each year and followed by a parent-teacher conference (in January and June), are part of our ongoing communications with parents. Two other parent-teacher conferences are held (the September Intake conference and a no-report November conference), as well as a Portfolio Night in the spring. In addition, teachers send home a weekly letter to their students' parents (I also send home a weekly letter) and parents are invited throughout the year to assist in classrooms and join us when students present their PEPs.

Portfolio Night

Keeping a portfolio for each child—a collection of work and artifacts that give a picture of the child's growth—is a way of capturing progress without using paper and pencil measures. Unless the portfolio is given credence and shared with parents as a report card is, however, it will be seen as just a grab-bag with little educational significance. At New City, the spring Portfolio Night highlights the role of the portfolio.

During Portfolio Night, parents and children review student artifacts and reflections and put their hands on evidence of student growth. Families come together to celebrate student progress and accomplishments and to talk about areas needing more attention and effort. In short, reviewing portfolios gives parents an opportunity to view their children's progress in all of the intelligences.

The teacher's role in Portfolio Night is simply to welcome parents and to be available for questions. Because student reflection plays such a key role in the value of portfolios, it is important that the students review the contents of their portfolios with

their parents. Portfolios contain achievements, but they also hold work in progress and sometimes work that is noteworthy because of a lack of success. Indeed, "processfolios" is a better term to describe the purpose of a portfolio.

All items in a portfolio should contain a reflection sheet, such as the one in Figure 4.2 (p. 30). Completed by students, teachers, or both, these forms indicate the particular intelligence or intelligences an item addresses and why it was chosen for the portfolio. Without reflection sheets, it is easy for objects to lose their significance over time. Photographs of three-dimensional accomplishments as well as audiotapes and videotapes that capture a student's progress should also be included in each portfolio. Portfolios should be cumulative, being passed on from grade to grade; however, it is a good idea to cull the portfolio each spring, deciding which objects are representative and should remain and which items can be sent home with the students. As a group, the staff can decide whether portfolios should contain evidence of accomplishments that occur outside school, such as scouting activities, athletics, or musical performances.

School Displays

If advertising has taught us anything, it is that images can send a powerful message. Think carefully about what is hanging on the walls and in the halls of the school. Are student successes in different intelligences shown? If an Honor Roll is posted, is it based only on the scholastic intelligences? Where is there evidence of students who have excelled in the personal intelligences? Does the art program have the same prominence as the athletic program?

It is helpful to have parents in the building as often as possible to see what is happening. We want parents in our building because we use our halls and walls for educating, not just decorating. Even if parents only come in the building at the start of the day (7:00 a.m.) or at the end of extended day (6:30

FIGURE 4.1
Sample Progress Report on Logical-Mathematical Intelligence

Name **Paul**

LOGICAL-MATHEMATICAL INTELLIGENCE

4th Grade ☒ Fall ☐ Spring

/ = Not assessed at this time

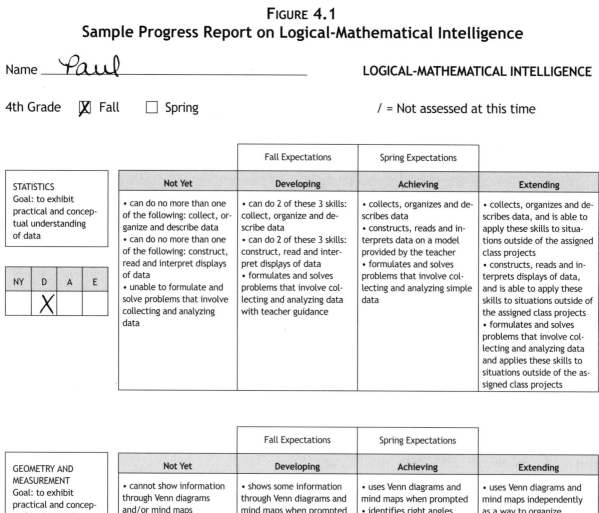

STATISTICS		Fall Expectations	Spring Expectations	
Goal: to exhibit practical and conceptual understanding of data	Not Yet	Developing	Achieving	Extending
	• can do no more than one of the following: collect, organize and describe data • can do no more than one of the following: construct, read and interpret displays of data • unable to formulate and solve problems that involve collecting and analyzing data	• can do 2 of these 3 skills: collect, organize and describe data • can do 2 of these 3 skills: construct, read and interpret displays of data • formulates and solves problems that involve collecting and analyzing data with teacher guidance	• collects, organizes and describes data • constructs, reads and interprets data on a model provided by the teacher • formulates and solves problems that involve collecting and analyzing simple data	• collects, organizes and describes data, and is able to apply these skills to situations outside of the assigned class projects • constructs, reads and interprets displays of data, and is able to apply these skills to situations outside of the assigned class projects • formulates and solves problems that involve collecting and analyzing data and applies these skills to situations outside of the assigned class projects

NY	D	A	E
	X		

GEOMETRY AND MEASUREMENT		Fall Expectations	Spring Expectations	
Goal: to exhibit practical and conceptual understanding of geometry and measurement	Not Yet	Developing	Achieving	Extending
	• cannot show information through Venn diagrams and/or mind maps • does not recognize an angle • does not recognize similar, congruent and symmetrical shapes • attempts to calculate area and perimeter with limited success • identifies plane and space figures • rarely identifies parallel, perpendicular and intersecting lines	• shows some information through Venn diagrams and mind maps when prompted • recognizes that two lines form an angle • identifies similar, congruent and symmetrical shapes • calculates area and perimeter • identifies and classifies plane and space figures • sometimes identifies parallel, perpendicular and intersecting lines	• uses Venn diagrams and mind maps when prompted • identifies right angles • identifies and creates similar, congruent and symmetrical shapes • understands and calculates area and perimeter • identifies, classifies and creates plane and space figures • identifies parallel, perpendicular and intersecting lines and line	• uses Venn diagrams and mind maps independently as a way to organize information • identifies right angles and can apply this concept to 3-dimensional figures • identifies and creates similar, congruent and symmetrical shapes and can apply these concepts to 3-dimensional figures • estimates area and perimeter accurately • creates plane and space figures to solve a problem • identifies parallel, perpendicular and intersecting lines, and can apply these concepts to 3-dimensional figures

NY	D	A	E
		X	

FIGURE 4.1—*continued*

Name _Paul_

LOGICAL-MATHEMATICAL INTELLIGENCE

4th Grade ☒ Fall ☐ Spring

/ = Not assessed at this time

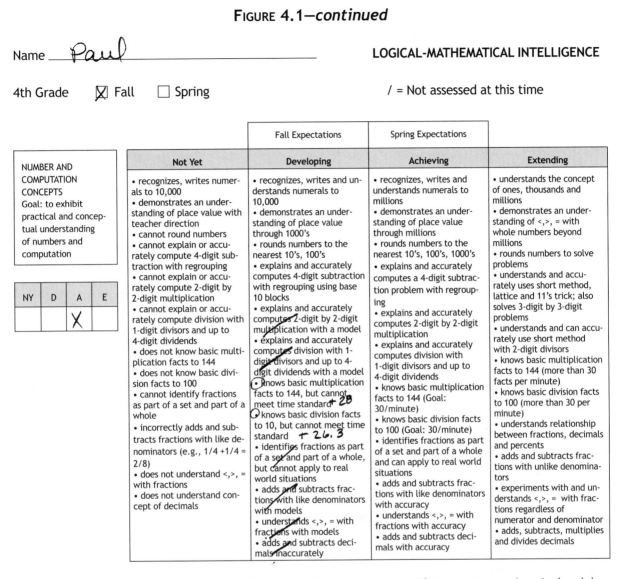

	Fall Expectations	Spring Expectations	
	Not Yet	**Developing**	**Achieving**	**Extending**
NUMBER AND COMPUTATION CONCEPTS Goal: to exhibit practical and conceptual understanding of numbers and computation	• recognizes, writes numerals to 10,000 • demonstrates an understanding of place value with teacher direction • cannot round numbers • cannot explain or accurately compute 4-digit subtraction with regrouping • cannot explain or accurately compute 2-digit by 2-digit multiplication • cannot explain or accurately compute division with 1-digit divisors and up to 4-digit dividends • does not know basic multiplication facts to 144 • does not know basic division facts to 100 • cannot identify fractions as part of a set and part of a whole • incorrectly adds and subtracts fractions with like denominators (e.g., 1/4 +1/4 = 2/8) • does not understand <,>, = with fractions • does not understand concept of decimals	• recognizes, writes and understands numerals to 10,000 • demonstrates an understanding of place value through 1000's • rounds numbers to the nearest 10's, 100's • explains and accurately computes 4-digit subtraction with regrouping using base 10 blocks • explains and accurately computes 2-digit by 2-digit multiplication with a model • explains and accurately computes division with 1-digit divisors and up to 4-digit dividends with a model • knows basic multiplication facts to 144, but cannot meet time standard +2B • knows basic division facts to 10, but cannot meet time standard +26.3 • identifies fractions as part of a set and part of a whole, but cannot apply to real world situations • adds and subtracts fractions with like denominators with models • understands <,>, = with fractions with models • adds and subtracts decimals inaccurately	• recognizes, writes and understands numerals to millions • demonstrates an understanding of place value through millions • rounds numbers to the nearest 10's, 100's, 1000's • explains and accurately computes a 4-digit subtraction problem with regrouping • explains and accurately computes 2-digit by 2-digit multiplication • explains and accurately computes division with 1-digit divisors and up to 4-digit dividends • knows basic multiplication facts to 144 (Goal: 30/minute) • knows basic division facts to 100 (Goal: 30/minute) • identifies fractions as part of a set and part of a whole and can apply to real world situations • adds and subtracts fractions with like denominators with accuracy • understands <,>, = with fractions with accuracy • adds and subtracts decimals with accuracy	• understands the concept of ones, thousands and millions • demonstrates an understanding of <,>, = with whole numbers beyond millions • rounds numbers to solve problems • understands and accurately uses short method, lattice and 11's trick; also solves 3-digit by 3-digit problems • understands and can accurately use short method with 2-digit divisors • knows basic multiplication facts to 144 (more than 30 facts per minute) • knows basic division facts to 100 (more than 30 per minute) • understands relationship between fractions, decimals and percents • adds and subtracts fractions with unlike denominators • experiments with and understands <,>, = with fractions regardless of numerator and denominator • adds, subtracts, multiplies and divides decimals

NY	D	A	E
		X	

COMMENTS: Research shows that place value issues constitute 70% of errors in computation. Because of this, time was spent on place value through the billions, as well as subtraction. Base ten blocks provided students with a concrete method of exploration. Paul scored 90% on a subtraction review and 97% on a place value review. Paul is also close to achieving a +30 fourth-grade goal on the Mad Minutes. Yea!

While we were reading *Shiloh*, we recreated his 6′ x 8′ pen on the classroom floor. This led to our exploration of area and perimeter. Students used geoboards, dot paper, and other manipulatives to look at these concepts.

The elections provided statistics galore. Students were introduced to the concepts of percents and averages. The first step was to find percents and averages using a calculator. As we continue to look at these concepts throughout the year, we'll work toward better understanding the process. Information from the elections was also shown in pie and line graphs. Other statistics were used to create bar graphs. On a recent review, Paul was able to show proficiency in all areas except on labeling a bar graph properly. Paul seems to enjoy learning about and messing with statistics.

Effort in developing Mathematical Intelligence: AC   DA   (ED)

Carla
_____
Teacher

Fall Fact Information:

Your child has mastered multiplication and division facts through the 12's using the individualized Math Magician Program.   (yes)   no

+ _26.8_ Average number of subtraction facts completed per minute. (+30 is the 4th grade goal; anyone averaging over +30 is above grade level.)

FIGURE 4.2
New City School Portfolio Reflection

Name _____

Title of Work _____
(or description)

Date _____

Grade Level _____

Teacher _____

This work exhibits my efforts in the following Multiple Intelligences area(s):
❑ Bodily-Kinesthetic
❑ Interpersonal
❑ Intrapersonal
❑ Linguistic
❑ Logical-Mathematical
❑ Musical
❑ Naturalist
❑ Spatial

Note: I submitted this work under the intelligence I have checked in the list above.

Reflection and Comments:

_____

_____

_____

_____

_____

p.m.), we have an opportunity to educate them. We need to create an environment where parents are comfortable. At New City, a giant coffee urn sits in the main hall beneath a sign that invites parents to have a cup of coffee and linger with us! Whether a parent has time to stop for a cup of coffee, whether a parent even drinks coffee, the message is that parents are welcome in our school.

When parents visit, they see student work of all kinds prominently displayed throughout our halls. Line-autobiographies (personal life stories told spatially and logically-mathematically through a line graph) are posted next to T-shirt book reports (large pieces of paper shaped like a T-shirt, featuring a drawing that captures the essence of the book, plus a narrative). Dioramas of Native American tribes sit next to definitions of what all families, modern and ancient, have in common, and adjacent to student illustrations of emotions. To give younger students an understanding of how to record data, a poster with a row of nails indicates the possible number of siblings in a family. Each student then hangs a giant paper clip under the number of siblings that matches her family, thus creating a bar graph made up of various lengths of paper clip chains. Other classes create full-size three-dimensional bodies, lungs made of balloons and bones of white Styrofoam packing material, which they hang from the walls. Issues of race and data collection come together in a bar-graph chart that reads "My skin color looks like . . ." Students print their name above the appropriate substance: brown sugar, bran flakes, oatmeal.

The hanging of student work, however well done or attractive, is not sufficient. Parents need explanations. In our halls you will find explanations by the student work, showing parents, *educating* parents, what we are doing and why it has value. Here is an example of a posted explanation from our halls:

The 4th grade has been getting to know about the life and work of Frida Kahlo, a female artist from Mexico. Frida led a fascinating, but often very difficult, life. Most of her paintings are self-portraits that she began very early in her career. Often her self-portraits include some imagery that symbolizes various circumstances in her life, such as the accident she was involved in or her marriage. We tried to show personal depth in these self-portraits by our 4th graders by using strong contrast in the foreground and background, and using images and symbols that represent our likes and dislikes. Look carefully, as there is often more here than is obvious!

Surrounding the description are self-portrait collages done by the students.

On another floor, the following explanation is hung:

SPATIAL ANALYSIS OF A POEM

The 5th grade has finished reading *The Outsiders* by S. E. Hinton. A Robert Frost poem, "Nothing Gold Can Stay," appears in the book. We talked about the meaning of the poem as it stands alone and also its meaning within the context of *The Outsiders*. Students were asked to create a spatial analysis of the poem within the context of the story.

Student art work, a spatial analysis of their interpretation of the poem, is posted around the explanation.

Parent Education

An important part of parent education is also educating parents about our use of standardized tests. We may not like the fact that some decisions are made based on percentiles and stanines, and we may believe the tests have little validity; however, standardized tests are the gatekeepers of the educational establishment and it is important not only that our students perform well on these types of tests, but that our parents know that we expect our students to do what is needed to excel. As a result, we work on test-taking skills, remind parents about the importance of a good breakfast (especially during testing week), and report the information to parents in an understandable manner.

But again, if the only information shared with parents is a traditional report card that focuses on the scholastic intelligences and the results of standardized tests, the message to parents is that these are the only intelligences that truly have value. Looking at all of the intelligences, determining which need to have more prominence, and then deciding how to report on these intelligences can powerfully influence both students and their parents.

Reaching the Community

Inviting outsiders—parents, grandparents, friends, individuals with expertise—to witness students' presentations, exhibitions, and presentations (PEPs) is a good way to prepare students for experiences outside the classroom and to help educate the larger community about student progress. Inviting students from other classes to attend PEPs also gives student presenters an appropriate audience and lets those in the audience understand what is expected from them, too, if they are asked to perform a similar task.

Intake Conferences

Another effective strategy that works in a MI environment is an intake conference. Too often schools talk and parents are expected to listen. Although that shouldn't be acceptable in any school, it makes even less sense in a MI school where many intelligences are pursued out of school in the evenings and on weekends. An early Intake Conference

(perhaps in lieu of a fall parent and teacher conference) in which the expectation is that parents will talk most of the time and teachers will listen most of the time enables teachers to learn about their students' interests and strengths in the various intelligences. It also tilts the power relationship between teachers and parents as it is based on the premise that parents have expertise and can offer useful information about their children.

✦ ✦ ✦

For Faculty Discussion

1. Walking through the halls of our school, which intelligences are honored?
2. Which intelligences do we highlight in our reporting and communications to parents? Which are not given much attention?
3. How do students reflect on their performances and understanding?
4. How do we educate our students' parents about our program and values?

Steps to Implementing MI

Each school and each MI journey is different. Here are some tips to help you in your pursuit of MI.
1. Form a faculty committee to look at assessment, both what is measured and how it is measured. How could the report cards be redesigned or recreated to ensure that the value of MI is communicated to both students and parents?
2. Explore using teacher portfolios as a way to help faculty members see the merit of the portfolios.
3. Plan culminating student presentations and performances so that they are done before an audience of "outsiders." Invite parents and community members to the school to serve as this audience.

5 | CREATIVE ROUTES TO MI

Many educators embrace MI because it respects the role of the teacher. MI allows educators to know their students, to identify the ways they learn, and to be creative in creating curriculum and assessment tools. MI can be a powerful tool in helping students learn skills and acquire understandings. For MI to make a difference in students' learning, it should be used regularly and integrated into the school day, not viewed as an extra or a special occurrence. MI can be used with a variety of instructional strategies, such as lectures, learning centers, projects and exhibitions, and as part of cooperative learning activities. Teachers can use MI to help students learn and students can use it to show what they have learned. A single teacher can use MI in the classroom, or it can be a part of schoolwide endeavors. No matter who uses MI, it should be entwined in the culture.

Dispelling MI Myths

The flexibility of implementing MI presents some drawbacks. Because MI is not a set curriculum, because each educator or group of educators can fashion an approach that fits the particular context, the idea of MI is vulnerable to misinterpretation and misapplication. Before suggesting some promising ways to integrate MI into a school's program, I'd like to alert you to some potential trouble spots.

• MYTH: *Each intelligence should be incorporated in every lesson.* Although an occasional lesson might have eight options, addressing each intelligence in every lesson fragments instruction and requires an incredible amount of planning and preparation time. Attempting to incorporate each intelligence in every lesson is unrealistic.

• MYTH: *Surrounding students with the various intelligences is a good way to address MI.* Merely exposing students to various intelligences, while laudable, is not the same as enabling them to use their intelligences in learning and sharing information. Music playing in the background is pleasant and walls adorned with fine art are always attractive. Neither condition, however, helps children use their array of intelligences in learning.

• MYTH: *There is significant merit in formally labeling each student's intelligence.* The intelligences should be thought of as *tools*, not as ends in themselves. To the degree that knowing a student's strengths helps educators plan and tailor instruction for that student, assessment in particular intelligences can be beneficial. But simply measuring and labeling a student's level of proficiency in an intelligence or in all intelligences serves no practical purpose and may lead to labeling or categorizing students. If formal assessment of intelligences is to be done, students should be assessed through their direct use of the intelligences.

• MYTH: *There is no need for students to understand the MI model and know how it is being used.* Knowing the intelligences is the first step in helping students recognize how they learn best, which intelligences are their strongest and, equally important, which intelligences are their weakest. Knowledge also plays an integral part in developing students' intrapersonal intelligence.

• MYTH: *Children should always be allowed to choose which intelligences they wish to pursue.* Although there is merit in letting students select the intelligences in which they wish to work—they typically choose their strongest intelligences—educators are responsible for helping students grow in all intelligences and learn the best ways to solve problems.

Integrating MI in the Classroom

Creative teachers find opportunities to tailor their curriculum and instructional approaches to allow students to use different intelligences to learn and to share what they understand. As students become more comfortable using their various intelligences, they may solve problems or display knowledge using an intelligence not anticipated by the teacher. Establishing a classroom climate where students feel free to take risks and use different intelligences is an important hallmark of incorporating MI. Even granting that all lessons can have multiple pathways to learning, available time and energy simply do not allow for all lessons to incorporate all of the intelligences. Some lessons will remain single-intelligence lessons. What, then, are some useful approaches to incorporating MI into lessons and the classroom?

Curriculum-based Learning Centers

These centers use a specific intelligence to address a skill or understanding. If the class has just completed reading a novel, for example, the teacher might design a series of centers, each corresponding

to a particular intelligence, to determine the students' understanding of what they have read. The directions at a spatial center might ask students to draw a series of pictures or cartoons (filmstrip-like) to show what they have read and learned. A math center might ask students to create a line graph to show the story's rising action and denouement. The activity at the linguistic center might be to show understanding of character by telling (speaking into a tape recorder) or writing how a particular character viewed a situation; or students might be asked to change the situation and project how a character would respond. A bodily-kinesthetic center might require students to dramatize significant events in the story.

After reading *Julie of the Wolves*, for example, students might be asked to plot Julie's trek across the Canadian wilderness on a map that they create; or they might draw a series of cells to create a cartoon strip, showing how Julie foraged for food. A line graph could capture Julie's emotions as she was lost, feared for her life, became resolute in her desire to find civilization, and ultimately succeeded in completing her journey. Students could keep a journal of her journey; the journal could be written, audiotaped, or drawn. Other learning centers might ask students to choose among musical selections to capture the action in the story or to work as a group to create or perform a play that features part of the story. The range of possibilities is practically endless, but using centers provides students with opportunities to use different intelligences to show what they have learned about a specific curriculum focus or goal. These centers are generally short-term and address a particular aspect of the curriculum by offering opportunities for reinforcement, extension, and assessment of skills or understandings.

Intelligence-based Learning Centers

Intelligence-based learning centers are designed to enable a student to pursue some of the skills related to a particular intelligence. They are typically used less frequently than the curriculum-based learning centers and differ from them in that they are not tied to a specific curriculum focus or goal; the intent is to help students develop the particular intelligence. When intelligence-based learning centers are used, teachers design centers for all of the intelligences, each containing many different activities. A spatial center, for example, might offer students the option of drawing a picture, solving a maze, or using a mind-map to share information. Or students may be given opportunities to use photos or magazine pictures to create a collage that expresses an emotion. Sometimes students might be asked to use several different forms of spatial intelligence in capturing the same event or an emotion. For example, students might paint a picture, create a collage, and draw a mind-map to describe how they think Native Americans felt when they first encountered explorers from Europe.

A musical center might have a cassette player and earphones and ask students to select music that best captures the mood of the historical event they are studying. Students might be asked to compose a musical piece or write lyrics to a tune they have been given.

One teacher created a center with several tape recorders and headphones, each featuring a different genre of music (jazz, blues, rock and roll, classical). After the class discussed different kinds of music and how they are used, students listened to the various kinds of music and wrote words or drew pictures to share how the music made them feel. As a culminating activity, the teacher hung a sheet over a clothesline strung across the classroom and turned off the lights. The students sat on one side of the "curtain" as each student took a turn as the performer. The performer, silhouetted against the curtain with a powerful flashlight shining behind him, chose a musical selection and, using headphones, danced or moved to the music. The

audience, unable to hear the music, was to identify the kind of music the performer was listening to based only on his movements.

Depending on what resources are available (including space), several centers focused on a single intelligence may be available, or just one center for each intelligence. Again, while reinforcement of skills or assessing understanding is important, the primary goal of these centers is to give students experiences to enable them to develop their intelligences. These centers generally have activities that take students longer to complete than those in curriculum-based centers, and offer more complex tasks.

In working with either kind of center, students may be given the option to choose a center, they may be assigned one or more centers, or they may need to follow a plan or schedule that moves them through various centers. Alternating approaches, sometimes assigning centers and sometimes letting students select where they wish to work, seems to make the most sense.

When students are allowed to select intelligence-based centers, consider the degree to which their choices are influenced by factors other than the intelligence featured in the centers. A few years ago, for example, one of our teachers tried to test the hypothesis that when given options, students would go to the centers that allowed them to use their strongest intelligences. She observed the class for a few weeks in a variety of situations, in class and at recess, and recorded how the students spent their time, identifying each student's strongest intelligences. She then created intelligence-based centers and scheduled 30 minutes each day for students to work in the centers of their choice. Much to her amazement, there was little relationship between the intelligences she had identified as the students' stronger ones and the centers they selected. After a couple days of trying to figure out what was happening, she asked Adam, a student with strong bodily-kinesthetic talents and interests, why he was choosing to go to the music center. "Because that's where Fred goes," he replied. She told this story to me with no small amount of embarrassment, realizing that she had failed to anticipate that many students would base their choice on friendships more than intelligences. Of course, another way of looking at this is that Adam was being led by his interpersonal intelligence more than his bodily-kinesthetic intelligence.

A question we are often asked is "Do you help children develop their strongest intelligences or try to help them pull up their weakest intelligences?" The answer is that we try to do both. The value we place on MI and, as a result, the time that students spend engaging in the various intelligences means that students will become more proficient in many more of the intelligences than if our focus was only on the scholastic intelligences. That said, our intent is to use the intelligences as *tools* in helping our students learn. Regardless of the kind of center in which students are working, the experience is more meaningful if they are given the opportunity to reflect on their experience and, if applicable, how they worked with others.

Projects, Exhibitions, and Presentations

Projects, exhibitions, and presentations (PEPs) apply a performance perspective to MI. Students *use* their intelligences to share what they know with a wider audience. For example, students create a diorama that shows a scene from a novel or shows how a tribe of Native Americans lived, thereby using their spatial and bodily-kinesthetic (small-motor muscles) intelligences to depict what they know. Similarly, students use a variety of intelligences to prepare a display that shows how the human body functions, how plants grow, or how a snake sheds its skin.

If the student-created artifacts are accompanied by an oral presentation, the students also use interpersonal, linguistic, and, perhaps, the bodily-kinesthetic intelligences. Preparing for an "unknown" audience, whether students from other grades or adults, raises the stakes a bit and encourages students to be clear in both their understanding and presentation. Each 3rd grader, for example, researches a Native American tribe and creates a diorama representing some aspect of that tribe's life. On presentation day, the students stand next to their dioramas, ready to talk about the diorama and the tribe with other students and adults. Similarly, our 4th graders select one of the 50 states and give oral and written presentations featuring a description of the state along with graphs, drawings, and examples of typical food grown and eaten in the area.

Afterward, students reflect on their performance, ranging from simply responding to "What would you do differently?" to soliciting feedback from the audience, to watching a videotape of their performance. Reflection is an integral tool in developing intrapersonal intelligence. Inviting parents and community members to presentations is a wonderful way to educate them about the effectiveness of MI because it lets them see how students use a variety of intelligences to learn.

Thematic Instruction

The premise of thematic instruction is that students learn best when learning is meaningful. A theme is a unifying concept that transcends disciplines and content areas; at New City School, themes typically are studied for a semester or a full year. Instead of the curriculum being a series of unrelated skills and pieces of content to be learned, it is related to and derived from the theme. After a theme is chosen, the teachers create a curriculum that addresses agreed-upon skills and understandings. Because the themes are selected and developed by teachers, often in conjunction with their students, the themes are interesting, relevant, and easily converted into projects, exhibitions, and presentations that can be done individually or collaboratively. Thematic instruction supports the use of MI and vice versa.

The rich possibilities of thematic instruction can be seen in the 4th grade theme, "Citizens Make a Difference," which serves to transform the classroom into a government, with students acting as alderpeople and the teacher serving as mayor. Laws are proposed and passed to regulate classroom conduct. During the year the classes go to St. Louis's City Hall and Jefferson City, the state capital, to see where laws are made and city and state government takes place. How we can make a difference by taking personal responsibility is addressed in many ways, from a disabilities unit in which students either spend a day in a wheelchair, blindfolded, or have their dominant arm bound, to focusing on how they can listen to others and respond to their needs. Homelessness has been addressed as part of this theme, and the director of a nearby homeless shelter has visited the class to talk about her job and the shelter. In addition, students visited the homeless shelter during the day (when it was empty) to help prepare food. (See Chapter 2 for more information on themes.)

Using MI in Schoolwide Endeavors

The linguistic, logical-mathematical, spatial, bodily-kinesthetic, musical, and naturalist intelligences are each closely related to a certain academic discipline. Because of the narrow way that schools typically approach curriculum and instruction, the value of any one of these intelligences may depend on where you are in the school building! In general, a student with a strong spatial intelligence shines in the art room, a student with bodily-kinesthetic intelligence finds success in the gym or on the playground, while a student with musical intelligence flourishes in the music room or on stage. In the science lab or outdoors, a student with a proclivity to

the naturalist intelligence excels, and students with strong linguistic and logical-mathematical intelligences do well in writing, language, and math classes. Confining students to using specific intelligences in specific disciplines and certain areas of the school limits their opportunities for success.

Students should be able to use their array of intelligences to learn in all disciplines and in every classroom. Regardless of what they are expected to teach, all teachers should seek for students to capitalize on their MI strengths. Our experience has taught us that in addition to looking for ways to incorporate MI into individual classrooms, it is valuable to create schoolwide opportunities for students to tap into their intelligences so that they become more knowledgeable about and develop their intelligence strengths. Using MI schoolwide not only gives students more chances to flourish, it heightens the visibility of the intelligences, sending a powerful message to the school community that all of the intelligences are valued. What follows are some ideas for using MI in schoolwide endeavors.

The Flow Room

Are there times when you skipped meals or missed appointments because you were so involved in an activity that you lost track of time? If so, you probably were successfully meeting a challenge that you enjoyed. Whether immersed in writing a letter, pruning flowers, achieving a personal best on your exercise machine, composing or performing a song, or putting the final piece in the hand-carved model of the *Titanic*, you were in *flow*, "the state in which people are so involved in an activity that nothing else seems to matter" (Csikszentmihalyi, 1990, p. 4). Because we are most likely to find our flow when we are using our strongest intelligences to respond to a difficult and interesting problem, flow can be associated with using MI. It is when athletes are pushing their bodies, writers are lost in narrative, and painters are creating a new reality on an easel—when they are accomplishing through their strongest intelligences—that flow is found.

Unfortunately, schools are so linguistically and logically-mathematically based that some students spend most of the school day using the intelligences that are not their strongest. A flow room gives students options to pursue what they do best and enables them to use their stronger intelligences. It is stocked with a range of materials that correspond to the various intelligences and students are allowed to choose their activity and choose if they want to work by themselves or with others. Students typically work with little adult direction or intervention. Whether they are playing chess or Twister, building a model alone or with a friend, listening to or performing music, painting, classifying a collection of insects, or writing in a journal, they are probably involved in an activity in which they are succeeding, one that allows them to use their intelligence strengths. Citing chess, tennis, and poker as examples of activities that can create a sense of flow, Csikszentmihalyi says that flow takes place when both goals and the appropriate responses are clear. Of course, opportunities for students to pursue flow can be created within classrooms, in the hall or lunchroom, or outside the school. All that is needed is a range of options that corresponds to the intelligences and opportunities for students to get involved and become engaged.

Many students, particularly those who are not strong in the scholastic intelligences, go for long periods of time without finding success, without realizing flow. For them, flow does not happen at school; if flow takes place, it happens after school or over the weekend. Flow may not happen for some children if family resources are limited and a child is not able to take lessons or have opportunities to play on teams. Some children become adults without experiencing flow; not having experienced it, these adults do not know what they are missing. For too many children and adults, the closest they come to experiencing flow is the passive sensation they get from sitting in front of a television or computer screen for hours at a time.

A flow room—any flow space, really—is most effective when it does more than just allow students to enjoy themselves and use their stronger intelligences. An important aspect of flow is the opportunity that it presents for helping students reflect on and become aware of their stronger intelligences and how they find enjoyment. Teachers can help students consciously learn about their interests and the pursuit of flow by asking them to reflect on their feelings after they have engaged in tasks associated with different intelligences. Do they find, for example, that they are more refreshed after playing chess than after finishing a drawing? Does listening to music or playing hopscotch cause them to forget about some of the day's frustrations? Are they able to focus their energies on building a model or watching a mouse in a cage regardless of the distractions in the room? Are they more "productive" when working alone or as a member of a team?

Students who are strong intrapersonally have a sense of how their participation in various tasks (corresponding to the various intelligences) relates to their moods and feelings, whether or not questions are posed to them about this. For those students who are not very strong intrapersonally, however, the issue needs to be raised directly. Ask students to keep track of the frequency and time they spend engaging in various activities. A more elaborate approach is to have them record their feelings on a Likert-type scale ("strongly agree," "agree," etc.) before and after they participate in activities. Reviewing the data with students can help them discern tendencies and patterns in their behavior and learn about themselves.

Understanding ourselves, developing the intrapersonal intelligence, enables us to gain control over our feelings. In *Emotional Intelligence*, Daniel Goleman says, "Much of what we do—especially in our free time—is an attempt to manage mood. Everything from reading a novel or watching television to the activities and companions we choose can be a way to make ourselves feel better. The art of soothing ourselves is a fundamental life skill" (1995, p. 57). Experiences in a flow room, pursuing flow and learning about oneself, can help develop the intrapersonal intelligence.

Conversely, students should be encouraged to use the flow room to try different tasks and meet new challenges by investigating areas that do not correspond with their strengths. Although perhaps not as much fun as working with stronger intelligence and finding flow, exploring weaker intelligences also provides useful information to students about how they learn best, what causes difficulty, and how they can work at minimizing frustration. Working with the weaker intelligences is a valuable exercise in developing intrapersonal intelligence.

Learning Pods

In learning pods, gaining skill is the goal and students are often taught how to use an intelligence—how to mold clay, play an instrument, pot a plant, or kick a ball—through direct instruction. A specified time is set aside (perhaps an hour once or several times each week) and the entire school community offers unique, intelligence-oriented experiences. Often, all the adults in the building, including the office and custodial staff, serve as mentors and instructors for pods. Students choose an activity and pursue it for several sessions. Pods might focus on knitting or stitchery, table games, gardening, computers, architecture, music, cooking, sports, science experiments, magic tricks, public speaking, woodworking, or quiet reflection. As with flow rooms, pods offer students chances to pursue their stronger intelligences, find enjoyment, gain skill, and learn about themselves.

If it isn't possible to establish learning pods schoolwide, a teacher in one classroom or a few teachers working together can create these opportunities in their classrooms. Although fewer choices would be available, students would have opportunities to pursue and develop their intelligences.

Role Models

Role models can help to create enthusiasm for activities that require particular intelligences. Interacting with people whose roles are based on proficiency in the intelligences as they share their expertise and passion with students can help to widen students' horizons and aspirations. Whether visitors come to classrooms or perform in a schoolwide assembly, the result is the same: The students whose strongest intelligences correspond with those of the presenter will be touched and inspired in special ways. Schools that value MI should make special efforts to ensure that adults representing skill in each of the intelligences are visible and accessible to students. Likewise, taking students to locations where a high level of skill in specific intelligences is necessary—artists' studios, concerts, nature conservatories, sports competitions—is also important. With older students, creating mentor or apprenticeship programs or simply providing an opportunity for them to work directly with someone whose livelihood stems from proficiency in an intelligence can influence their lives. Presenting these kinds of role models is especially important if a school does not have music, physical education, and art teachers on staff or if students do not have regular access to the teachers of these subjects or intelligences.

Lengthening the School Day and School Year

Another approach to adding MI to an already full curriculum is through extending the school day and lengthening the school year. Adding more time for school does not mean more of the same. It means that schools can meet families' needs for after-school or summer supervision by providing opportunities for students to investigate and pursue different intelligences. As work patterns and families change, more schools are providing additional coverage for their students. At New City, for example, our school day is 8:30 a.m. to 3:30 p.m., but we offer coverage for our students from 7:00 a.m. until 6:30 p.m. The before-school coverage is free and is staffed primarily by teacher aides. As many as 150 of our 360 students stay after school in our fee-based Extended Day Program, which is primarily recreational in nature (although a study hall is offered for upper-grade students). College students are hired to work in this program.

Within the Extended Day Program, for an extra fee, we offer Talents Classes, sessions that meet weekly and are framed around MI. Adults, including some parents, teachers, and outsiders who use a particular intelligence as their livelihood, teach these classes. Recent offerings have included karate, drums, paper marbling, student newspaper, piano, jewelry making, insects and bugs, drama, photography, and Web page design. Perhaps my favorite offering was one that combined the musical and bodily-kinesthetic intelligences, Rock & Roll Roller Skating.

At New City School, we also offer a summer camp program for 10 weeks of the summer. All students go swimming each day, everyone gets to enjoy the flow room, and our older students have overnight camping trips. Extra classes are offered within the summer camp as well, including piano, drums, Web page design, writing, and mathematics. As with our Extended Day Program, the relatively leisurely pace of summer makes it a bit easier for us to allow our students to pursue their intelligences and find their flow.

Using MI requires more time and energy than does a traditional textbook-based approach to teaching, and political considerations and philosophical constraints can inhibit progress toward MI. But by being creative about MI, finding new ways to give kids opportunities to use all of their intelligences, students and teachers benefit. Learning centers, flow rooms, learning pods and looking anew at the school day and calendar can all be helpful in pursuing MI.

✦ ✦ ✦

For Faculty Discussion

1. Where in our school can kids pursue their non-scholastic intelligences?
2. What kinds of games and activities would go in our school's flow room?
3. How can we help students learn to understand and gain from their frustrations and failures?
4. How would we be different if our schools had valued MI when we were children?
5. How do we, the adults, find flow in our lives?

Steps to Implementing MI

Each school and each MI journey is different. The following tips, however, may be helpful in any pursuit of MI.

1. Begin discussing ways that MI could be addressed beyond what takes place in individual classrooms.
2. How could our school create MI opportunities for students before and after school, and during lunch?
3. Conduct an inventory of the talents and skills in various intelligences possessed by all the adults working or volunteering in our school. How could these be used to offer learning pods for students?
4. Plan a speakers series in which individuals embodying success in the various intelligences visit the school to share their passions and successes.

6 | THE IMPORTANCE OF THE PERSONAL INTELLIGENCES

When I give presentations on MI, I often begin by saying to the audience, "Take a moment and write down the initials of three adults you know personally and consider to be intelligent. How you define intelligence is up to you." I wait a moment and then ask the participants to write the initials of three famous people they consider to be intelligent. Finally I ask them to write the initials of three of their students they consider intelligent. Then I ask them to spend a few minutes discussing their answers in small groups, looking for both differences and similarities among the people on their lists. Finally, the small groups share their common people and characteristics with the whole group.

Regardless of the composition of the audience, whether educators or parents, whether the questions are asked in Maryland or Texas, Chile or Australia, the results are nearly the same. Rarely, if ever, are people identified solely because of their ability to read, write, or compute. Yes, those scholastic skills *are* important, to be sure, and many of the individuals on the lists possess them in abundance. But being able to read, write, and compute well are not in themselves qualities that prompt people to be identified by others as intelligent.

The consistent responses from a range of audiences indicate that proficiency in the scholastic intelligences (any of the intelligences, really) must be supplemented with strength in the personal intelligences. Simply put, if you can't work with others, if you continue to make the same mistakes, if your people skills are terrible, these deficiencies far outweigh your other skills and strengths. Writing, speaking, and calculating well are valuable threshold skills; these abilities give you access to a profession or role. Once there, however, accomplishment, advancement, and success come from knowing yourself and working successfully with others.

Perhaps in an earlier day, a lighthouse keeper could do a good job with little or no human interaction. The interconnectedness of today's society, however, means that working with others is an integral part of any complex task, and the prospect of technological advances only exacerbates the need to work together. Indeed, it may be that the personal intelligences are even more critical today because the speed at which information is generated and shared can leave little time for knowing and understanding others. For example, the use of e-mail is becoming pervasive because it speeds communication, but the use of e-mail reduces face-to-face human contact and interaction, inhibiting the relationship building that we need, particularly in times of stress. Writing about this phenomenon, Edward Hallowell (1999), talks about the "human moment: an authentic psychological encounter that can happen only when two people share the same physical space" and when emotional and intellectual attention is given to the other person. He says that "the absence of the human moment—on an organizational scale—can wreak havoc" (p. 60). The rarity of these human moments means that skill in the personal intelligences, the ability to work with others who are similar to and different from you, becomes even more critical. Preparing our students for this future means that it is essential that they can capitalize on their strengths and work well with others.

The gamut of multiple intelligences offers many different avenues for success and accomplishment, but in each the personal intelligences play an important role. Successful human interaction of any kind requires an ability to know oneself and to work with others. As Goleman writes in *Emotional Intelligence* (1995),

> Much evidence testifies that people who are emotionally adept—who know and manage their own feelings well, and who read and deal effectively with other people's feelings—are at an advantage in any domain of life, whether romance and intimate relationships or picking up the unspoken rules that govern success in organizational politics. People with well-developed emotional skills are also more likely to be content and effective in their lives, mastering the habits of mind that foster their own productivity; people who cannot marshal some control over their emotional life fight inner battles that sabotage their ability for focused work and clear thought (p. 36).

Someone who possessed exceptional interpersonal intelligence was Franklin D. Roosevelt. In discussing FDR in *No Ordinary Times* (1994), Goodwin says, "It seemed at times as if he possessed invisible antennae that allowed him to understand what his fellow citizens were thinking and feeling, so that he could craft his own responses to meet their deepest needs" (p. 78).

Years ago, a student named Jeffrey exemplified interpersonal intelligence. He was an avid chess player and played with the school counselor during weekly visits to work on overcoming his shyness. Jeffrey consistently beat her at chess and it was a standing joke between them. One day when they were finished meeting, the counselor came to me, exultant. "I beat Jeffrey in chess!" she said with a huge smile; he followed her, looking rather downtrodden. When the counselor left, I said to Jeffrey, "Boy, that's a surprise. She's never beaten you, has she?" He smiled at me and said, "I let her win because I knew she was having a bad day." In fact, the counselor was quietly going through the throes of a divorce and few people knew it. Jeffrey's keen interpersonal intelligence, however, alerted him to the fact that she was experiencing some difficulties, and he chose to help out by losing at chess.

A strong intrapersonal intelligence was displayed by one of our students, Adam, a couple of years ago when he was a 4th grader. His older sister, three years ahead of him, was linguistically gifted and had read nearly every book in our library before 6th grade. Adam struggled in learning to read and felt as if he was simply "Karen's younger brother" and not a very good student in comparison. As his class learned more and more about MI, however, he began to appreciate that the differences between them were just that, differences, not judgments of better or worse. One day his teacher came to me, almost teary-eyed with joy. "You won't believe what happened," she said. "We were talking about MI in class and Adam jumped up and said, 'I've got it! Karen is smart linguistically but I'm smarter logically-mathematically!'" She continued, "He then talked about the various intelligences and was able to identify the intelligences in which she was stronger but also those in which he excelled. I've been working so hard on building up his confidence and I think this was a breakthrough." As a result of his burgeoning intrapersonal intelligence, instead of feeling less smart than his linguistically talented sister, Adam was able to appreciate the areas in which he was strong while being aware of those areas that needed more attention.

The Unique Role of Intrapersonal Intelligence

During my presentations, after I have explained MI and focused on the personal intelligences, I often ask, "Is anyone a bad speller?" Despite the plethora of people with master's and doctorate degrees in the room, a forest of hands always appears before me. "It's not so important whether or not you can spell well today," I continue as some begin to nod, "and why is that?" Almost in unison the crowd responds "spell-check!"

"Yes," I continue, "but spell-check is helpful *only if you know you need to use it*, if you know you are a poor speller. This is where the intrapersonal intelligence comes in. Because if you don't know you spell badly, you'll continue to misspell, unaware, writing notes and turning in papers that are filled with errors." I continue, "Knowing that spelling is a weakness of yours, however, allows you to capitalize on spell-check or having someone else proof your work."

The point is that having a weakness isn't nearly as much of a problem as not knowing what the weakness is. If you don't know where you are weak, how can you systematically improve? Knowing ourselves—identifying and understanding what we do well and why we do it—is the intrapersonal intelligence.

The intrapersonal intelligence is the key intelligence. More than any other intelligence, a strong intrapersonal intelligence positions us for success; conversely, a weak intrapersonal intelligence likely means that we will continue to meet frustration and failure—and our successes, if we have any, will be random.

Knowing our strengths allows us to find situations in which what we do well is valued and where we can succeed. Knowing our weaknesses allows us to avoid situations where we are likely to fail (or at least we'll be aware of our weakness so that we can do what is necessary to succeed, as in using spell check). And knowing our weaknesses allows us to work at improving, to turn a weakness into a strength. Strong intrapersonal intelligence allows us to successfully navigate situations to capitalize on our strengths and minimize our weaknesses. Whatever our strengths and weaknesses, we can make the most of our talents through our intrapersonal intelligence. Conversely, a weak intrapersonal intelligence causes us to continue to make the same mistakes and prevents us from learning how to solve problems or avoid them.

The Reciprocity of the Personal Intelligences

The lines between the intelligences can be fuzzy. A talented visual artist certainly possesses a strong spatial intelligence, for example, but she also possesses sufficient bodily-kinesthetic talent to enable her to fashion the clay or move the brush to convey her vision. But nowhere are the intelligences more intermingled than with the interpersonal and intrapersonal intelligences. Gardner recognized this in his foreword to the New City faculty's second book, *Succeeding with Multiple Intelligences* (1996), saying, "I have always felt that the personal intelligences are more closely related to one another than any other two sets of intelligences. . . . To a theorist, clarification of the relation between the intelligences remains important; for the practitioner, however, some attention to both is the primary mission" (p. viii).

People who are strong intrapersonally are aware of how others perceive them and are continually monitoring how they are received. They may not be doing so consciously, but it is this ability, whether dealing with children or peers, that allows them to always seem to say the right thing, to know when to offer comfort and when to remain firm. In describing the interrelationship of these intelligences Goleman says, "Empathy builds on self-awareness; the more open we are to our own emotions, the more skilled we will be in reading feelings" (1995, p. 96).

It is important to note this reciprocity because, as we shall see, activities that develop either of the personal intelligences often address both simultaneously. When our faculty first pursued MI we had wonderfully rich and lengthy discussions about whether it was possible to be strong in the interpersonal intelligence without being strong in the intrapersonal intelligence or vice versa. We ultimately decided, as Gardner implies, that the two are so closely related that success or deficiencies in one of the personal intelligences will support or hamper the other.

Emotional Intelligence

Appreciation for the personal intelligences received a great push forward with the publication and success of *Emotional Intelligence*. Goleman focused exclusively on the personal intelligences, discussing such qualities as "self-control, zeal and persistence, and the ability to motivate oneself" (p. xii). He used many examples to make the case that teaching skills in these areas will give students "a better chance to use whatever intellectual potential the genetic lottery may have given them" (p. xii).

Goleman cites Yale professor Peter Salovey, who classified the personal intelligences into five areas (p. 43):

1. *Knowing one's emotions.* Self-awareness—recognizing a feeling *as it happens*—is a keystone of emotional intelligence. Self-awareness is being aware of both our mood and our thoughts about that mood.

2. *Managing emotions.* Handling feelings so that they are appropriate is an ability that builds on self-awareness.

3. *Motivating oneself.* Marshaling emotions in the service of a goal is essential for paying attention, for self-motivation and mastery, and for creativity.

4. *Recognizing emotions in others.* Empathy, another ability that builds on emotional self-awareness, is the fundamental "people skill."

5. *Handling relationships.* The art of relationships is, in large part, skill in managing emotions in others.

Salovey's first three domains of emotional intelligence correspond with Gardner's conception of intrapersonal intelligence; the last two correspond with Gardner's conception of interpersonal intelligence.

After a group of the New City faculty read *Emotional Intelligence*, we decided to introduce Salovey's five components to everyone else on a fall afternoon at a faculty meeting. The meeting started as usual with bulletin board announcements. Next we were talking about plans for an upcoming parent evening and one of my assistants was using the overhead projector to present the plans. Suddenly, without warning, I blew up at her, "Betsy," I said, "your overheads are sloppy. Can't you take any pride in your work?"

Her eyes widened and she responded just as explosively, "There you go again, Tom, always criticizing. You know I've been under some stress and you ought to cut me some slack!"

"Slack?" I responded, now walking toward her and almost yelling, "You want slack, but if I don't stay on your case nothing will get accomplished. I'm tired of this," and I threw some papers I had been holding on the floor and stomped out of the room.

The room was quiet as teachers sat stunned, having witnessed two administrators at their worst.

After a few seconds Betsy announced, "Relax, this wasn't real! Tom and I may make one another crazy at times but this was all fake!"

I returned to the room in time to hear exhalations and see bodies relaxing. I added, "We wanted to introduce a new model for the personal intelligences to you and rather than simply talking about it, we thought a little role play might be fun!" Then I passed out a sheet listing Salovey's five components and definitions and asked teachers to look through it and identify which of these Betsy and I had lacked in our interaction. Someone muttered in a stage whisper, "ALL!" and everyone laughed.

In the subsequent large-group discussion I asked the faculty if we ever saw these sorts of behaviors in real settings with students or adults. Of course, we all agreed that we do. We then talked about how Salovey's model offers specificity about the personal intelligences and how we need to address each area through our curriculum and instruction so that we do not fall prey to our emotions. "Too often," I said, "we focus on content and coverage, not giving enough attention to the personal intelligences when thinking about and planning for student growth. If this happens, our students leave with a handicap."

Developing the Personal Intelligences in the Classroom

Many different activities can be used to address the intrapersonal and interpersonal intelligences in a classroom. Taking into account students' developmental readiness, teachers can establish a classroom norm in which students regularly reflect on how they are feeling, their role in the group, and the effect they are having on others. Begin by simply asking students, "How do you think you did on this task?" and "What could you do differently next time?" Initially, focus students on their own performance. Over time, students can be led to rating themselves on their work in a group and then comparing their perceptions with feedback on their performance solicited from the other group members. We use the Personal MI Profile (Figure 6.1) and Math Inventory (Figure 6.2, p. 47) to help us and our students. Other examples of forms that can be used to help students reflect on and develop their intrapersonal intelligence are included in Appendix C.

Activities that can help students gain intrapersonal intelligence include surveys (to enable students to see how they compare with others), autobiographies and journals (not necessarily solely linguistic), experience charts, portfolios, and goal setting and monitoring. Activities that can help students gain interpersonal intelligence include collaborative writing, group projects, panel discussions and debates, rubrics or rating sheets for assessing a performance collaboratively, role playing, and interviews. One teacher has the class watch a five-minute clip of a television show that she taped with the sound turned off. She then asks, "Who can tell me what was happening?" Some of the students can identify characters' feelings and motives almost as well as if they could hear them speak, but for others the lack of sound precludes their having any idea of what was happening. An activity like this one leads to a great lesson on body language and the nonverbal ways that we can "read" others.

Other teachers use "gallery walks" when students have finished writing stories. Completed "best" student work is displayed, and other students read and critique it. For peer critiques to be successful, of course, the teacher must first teach the students how to give and receive feedback. Indeed, if students are to develop their personal intelligences, it is critical that teachers structure situations in which students give one another feedback on how each is performing as a member of the group. Feedback needs to be given carefully so that the students whose personal intelligences are the most lacking neither damage others' feelings nor are hurt themselves. As with so many other issues, time is an

FIGURE 6.1
Personal Multiple Intelligences Profile

Name: _____ _____ __ Date: _____

How much do you use each intelligence?
Put an X on the line to show how often you use each intelligence.

Interpersonal

Seldom   Sometimes   Often

Intrapersonal

Seldom   Sometimes   Often

Bodily-Kinesthetic

Seldom   Sometimes   Often

Linguistic

Seldom   Sometimes   Often

Logical-Mathematical

Seldom   Sometimes   Often

Musical

Seldom   Sometimes   Often

Naturalist

Seldom   Sometimes   Often

Spatial

Seldom   Sometimes   Often

Figure 6.2
Math Inventory

Name: _____ Date: _____

1. I think math is _____

because _____ .

2. My favorite math topic is _____

because _____ .

3. The math skill that is easiest for me is _____

_____ .

4. The math skill that is most difficult for me is _____

_____ .

Rate the following statements using this scale:

0	1	2	3	4	5	6	7	8	9	10
not at all										very much

Statement	Rating
5. I enjoy math.	____
6. I am enthusiastic about learning new math skills.	____
7. I use math skills in other subject areas.	____
8. The math skills I learn in school are useful to me when I am not in school.	____
9. I use my personal best effort in math.	____
10. I am good at math activities.	____

On the back of this sheet, list all the times you use math skills during the day.

important consideration. If students are going to reflect on their performance and their work with others, they need time to do the reflection.

Proactive Approach with Parents

As you focus your students on the personal intelligences, be aware that parents may be wary of your work, perhaps even more so than with the spatial, musical, naturalist, or bodily-kinesthetic intelligences. From a parent's perspective, the personal intelligences might seem to be related to values, and some parents will therefore worry that the school is impinging upon their parental responsibility to teach right and wrong. As mentioned in Chapter 2, parent education and parent understanding are essential to a successful MI program, and educators should take extra care in addressing the personal intelligences.

You can make a strong case that schools play a vital role in the development of children's personal intelligences, as skill in the personal intelligences is essential in *any* profession. In *Working with Emotional Intelligence* (1998), Goleman notes

> People are beginning to realize that success takes more than intellectual excellence or technical prowess, and that we need another sort of skill just to survive—and certainly to thrive—in the increasingly turbulent job market of the future. Internal qualities such as resilience, initiative, optimism, and adaptability are taking on a new valuation (p. 10).

By relating the personal intelligences to their success in the adult world—perhaps using the questions about identifying intelligent people that opened this chapter—parents can come to understand the importance of the personal intelligences, though the term is probably not familiar to them. Although parents can and do disagree about values, all parents want their children to succeed. Every parent has encountered difficulties with a colleague, friend, or boss; and at some level, every parent knows the importance of people skills in work and social settings. Once parents understand what the personal intelligences are, they are usually eager for their children to develop these skills.

Developing the Faculty's Personal Intelligences

Teachers and administrators also need to be conscious of and work toward developing their own personal intelligences. They need to learn to be aware of how they are feeling and how they affect others. Although work on the personal intelligences does not have to be part of every faculty meeting, it should be a priority. After all, staff are in effect modeling behavior for students.

A few years ago, in an effort to increase our faculty's intrapersonal intelligence and to encourage staff to think about our interpersonal intelligence, we began an August inservice day with a different kind of activity. After coffee and doughnuts, our 40 faculty members gathered in the amphitheater. One of my assistants, Nancy, began the presentation. She said, "Who we are, formed in part by our backgrounds, has a strong influence on how we view issues and how we work with one another and with our students. Sometimes we're aware of these things and sometimes we're not.

"What we're going to do now," Nancy continued, "is ask you some questions that will cause you to self-identify and group yourselves by how you respond. Each time, after I give you the categories and you physically move to a point to stand with others who share this particular characteristic, I'd like you to look around and note your position, individually, and the size of your group in comparison with the rest of the groups. Then I'll ask you some questions. After that, the groups will talk for a few minutes."

People weren't quite sure what was going to happen, but she went ahead anyway. "First,"

Nancy said, "I want you to stand in groups to indicate your strongest intelligence. When I finish naming them, let's have those who are strongest in the linguistic intelligence stand over here, behind me. Those who are strongest in spatial should move over there, across from me. If you're strongest in musical, then stand. . . . " She continued, listing all of the intelligences and indicating the different places where people should stand. Then, Nancy asked people to move. The groupings were fascinating. The linguistic group was largest, and the logical-mathematical group was smallest.

"OK, look around and note the size of the groups and who's in which group," she continued. "Are all of your teammates in the same group, or are you distributed among different intelligences? What does this mean?"

After giving the groups a minute or so to reflect and talk, Nancy asked everyone, "How does where you're standing, or the intelligence in which you're the strongest, affect your teaching?" This question led to a rich discussion within each group. After a couple minutes she announced that we were going to return to one large group and begin the process again. This time people were asked to sort themselves by their weakest intelligence, and the questions were repeated.

We continued this process four more times. People were asked to reclassify and group themselves according to their answers to the following questions.

• "How did your parents raise you? Were they strict, laissez-faire, or liberal?"
• "In what socioeconomic status were you raised? Wealthy, upper-middle class, middle class, lower-middle class, or poor?"
• "At what age did you first experience difficulties in school? During the elementary years, middle school years, high school, college, or never?"
• "At what age did you first work or play with others who were a different race from yourself?"

Again, after people had sorted themselves in response to each question, Nancy asked them to reflect on where they were in relation to the largest group, how the size their group compared with the other groups, who was in their group and what that might imply, and what their answer might suggest about their teaching. The activity ended with a final question to everyone, still standing in the last group: "What can you tell me about these questions? Why did we choose them and what do you note about the sequence in which they were asked?"

The discussions stemming from these questions and the groups in which we found ourselves were fascinating. Clearly, how we were raised, our school experiences, and our relations with other races powerfully affect who we are today and how we teach. Although some of us may have individually pondered these influences, most of us had not found the opportunity to share our thoughts with others, especially those with whom we are not very close. Doing so publicly validated that these factors need to be considered and opened the door to our talking about them in future formal and informal gatherings. We ended the activity by asking the faculty to form groups once again, this time by grade-level teams, to talk about how they felt during the process.

A single activity, even one as powerful as this, does not significantly move people forward in developing their personal intelligences. But a series of activities like this, supported by time to reflect on how we are feeling and how the group is working at committee, faculty, and ad hoc meetings, can go a long way toward setting a tone that helps advance everyone's personal intelligences. Having these experiences with our peers means that we are more likely to see their worth and lead our students in similar kinds of reflection and sharing.

For Faculty Discussion

1. Think of individuals—students and adults—who have excelled because of their personal intelligences. Share those thoughts and successes in discussion.

2. Is it possible to have a strong intrapersonal intelligence without a strong interpersonal intelligence? Is the opposite possible?

3. Think of the students who have difficulty succeeding in our school. Which of Salovey's five components do most of them lack?

4. What are some obstacles to focusing on the personal intelligences in our school?

Steps to Implementing MI

Just as each school is different, so is each MI journey.

There are, however, some steps that may be helpful in any pursuit of MI.

1. Hold a parent meeting and focus on the personal intelligences. Begin by presenting Gardner's model and Salovey's components. Perhaps distribute this article by Daniel Goleman: "What Makes A Leader?" from the November–December 1998 issue of *Harvard Business Review*.

2. Review how the personal intelligences are addressed in our school's grading system. How *could* they be addressed? What opportunities are there for students to develop or exhibit skills in these areas?

3. Convene a faculty committee to plan activities to help the faculty develop their personal intelligences. If this is too big a step, the committee can plan activities to help develop their own personal intelligences.

THE PERSONAL INTELLIGENCES ARE AMORAL

Gardner has said that the personal intelligences are amoral. That is, someone with a strong interpersonal intelligence could use the knowledge to do good or evil. Adolf Hitler no doubt possessed a strong interpersonal intelligence. Likewise, someone with a strong intrapersonal intelligence could use this self-knowledge to place herself in positions where her strength could be used to either help or harm others.

Clearly, focusing on the personal intelligences without also addressing values and morals is insufficient. In *The Moral Intelligence of Children*, Robert Coles (1997) notes that it is not enough for children to know right from wrong; they must act in the right way. In defining "moral intelligence," Coles refers to what a pediatrician friend told him "about girls and boys he'd known and treated who had it—who were 'good,' who were kind, who thought about others, who extended themselves toward those others, who were 'smart' that way" (p. 4). Even in a contentious setting, one in which parents argue about the merits of new math versus old math or phonics versus whole language, all parents want their children to possess these qualities described by Coles.

If we are to focus on helping students develop their personal intelligences, as I believe we must, we also have a responsibility to help them learn the difference between right and wrong. It is not enough to teach students how to understand themselves and others; we must also teach how to care for themselves and others and how to work with one another. That teaching must begin in the early grades. A practice as simple as asking young children "use your words," instead of crying, is valuable and effective when coupled with activities that help children begin to understand the effect their words and actions can have on other people.

In the primary grades at New City School, we use red chairs as a tool to teach students diplomacy and how to work with one another. Any student who feels that he has been verbally or physically abused or has had his feelings hurt by another child can summon the other person to the red chairs. There, seated and facing each other, under the direction of a teacher at the beginning of the school year, students learn to express their feelings and hear others. As they get older, students feel comfortable in summoning each other to the red chairs or being asked to join someone there without any adult intervention. Occasionally two children will ask to stay inside at recess to sit in the red chairs and work out a problem.

With that sort of preparation and understanding, the stage is set for older students to treat one another with care. No, our students are not angels, but they have learned to appreciate and respect each other, to treat others as they would like to be treated; they are sensitive to how their words and actions influence others.

Our efforts to have our students respect one another are reinforced by our practice of valuing racial, ethnic, and socioeconomic diversity. We focus on diversity in all we do, creating numerous entry points for discussion: from creating bar graphs with our preschoolers to tally their skin color, to taking the 5th grade on an overnight trip to the National Civil Rights Museum in Memphis. Believing in multiple intelligences supports our appreciation for diversity. All of this comes together to teach our children that every person is worthy of respect and that we can do well by doing good.

While our students have many talents and are smart in an array of intelligences, what gives us the most pride is when secondary school teachers say to us, "The students from New City are good kids, really nice to be around." We cannot, of course, take all of the credit for that; clearly, families greatly influence students' growth. But we believe our focus on the personal intelligences, coupled with our efforts to teach children empathy and respect for others, help facilitate the development of what Coles terms "moral intelligence."

7 | THE PHASES OF MI IMPLEMENTATION

Children pass through predictable stages of development as they grow, regardless of their culture or educational setting. Simply stated, a child must crawl before walking and walk before running. A child must count before adding and must know letters and sounds before reading.

The same developmental perspective that helps us understand children's growth offers insights about how organizations evolve. In *Corporate Lifecycles* (1988), Ichak Adizes says

> Organizations have lifecycles just as living organisms do; they go through the normal struggles and difficulties accompanying each stage of the Organizational Lifecycle and are faced with the transitional problems of moving to the next phase of development (p. xiii).

Just as it is important to know the developmental phases through which children evolve, understanding the developmental sequence of organizations can enable us to understand their growth and plan accordingly. Adizes says that "knowing where the organization [is] in the lifecycle enable[s] management to take proactive, preventive measures and deal with future problems earlier or avoid them altogether" (p. xiii). In *The Fifth Discipline* (1990), Peter Senge makes a similar comment, saying that recognizing the kinds of structures that recur again and again in organizations is a fundamental component of systems thinking.

Crooked Paths and Dead Ends

While a developmental lens is helpful in understanding any school's evolution, it is even more valuable when looking at schools experiencing the inevitable and significant changes that are part of becoming an MI school. Because the MI movement is a relatively new one and because there is no one formula for applying MI, the path to implementation will be crooked—and it will occasionally lead to dead ends.

New City School's Roadblocks

After 12 years of implementing MI, we still find ourselves progressing down crooked paths and running into dead ends. As difficult and disheartening as this can be, it isn't a negative experience. Rather, as the developmental model suggests, these frustrations are necessary steps in our progression.

A crooked path might best describe our use of portfolios. We have had a Portfolio Committee for years and have spent a great deal of time trying to use portfolios as a tool to help us document, understand, and assess student growth. We keep portfolios for students at every grade level and have a popular Portfolio Night in the spring (see Chapter

4), yet we are far from having a portfolio culture. After more than a decade, we still seem to view portfolios more as a collection of student artifacts than as tools that offer insights into student growth. We need to continue work on how we view and use portfolios.

Similarly, as hard as we work at parent education, pursuing it remains a crooked path. Although communication with parents has improved over the years, we still spend time undoing parent misperceptions. For example, a few years ago we altered our schedule and reallocated specialist teachers to offer more science time to our upper-grade students and more library time to our younger students. A parent who was uncomfortable with our use of MI told other parents that reallocation was done in response to our 6th graders' scoring poorly on a standardized science test. Although we had not given such a science test, and our students do quite well in science, this was a hot topic on the soccer sidelines and at the coffee pot in the hall. It took months for the canard to die. No doubt the rumor gained verisimilitude simply because using MI looks so different from a traditional approach to education. Even today we occasionally hear from parents who question the rigor of MI because their child thinks school is fun.

A very public dead end occurred not long after we announced, with great fanfare and hoopla, that we would use schoolwide themes to help us implement MI. Despite our enthusiasm, the idea was dismissed a few months later (see Chapter 2). And, after more than a year of investigating how a child's use of MI in the grade-level classroom could be captured by the creation of the MI Profile, the project was scrapped. The MI Profile sprung from the belief that what you measure is what you value and was intended to give an idea of a student's interest and proficiency in all of the intelligences. As originally designed, the MI Profile was to be shared with parents and facilitate and support classroom teachers' use of the intelligences.

Despite the fact that the MI Profile was created by a faculty committee, reviewed and modified by the remainder of the faculty, and included in our faculty's first book, we had problems. Just before we were to use the Profile, a group of teachers came to me, including some who had helped design it, and told me that they would be uncomfortable using it. Some teachers did not feel they could assess children in every intelligence, particularly those in which they themselves were not strong. Although it pained me to do so, I knew that I needed to respond to the teachers' concerns. Despite the scores of hours that were spent in preparation and despite my personal misgivings, the MI Profile was put aside. I hope some day to pull it from the ashes and have the faculty reconsider its use.

The MI Profile experience illustrates why we need to consider the strain that pursuing MI can have on a faculty. We must be realistic and accept the fact that implementing MI requires significant changes in the behavior of both teachers and administrators. Teachers who use MI move from being mere conveyers of information to acting as the professionals who develop curriculum, create assessment tools, work collegially with peers, and form new relationships with their students' parents. Administrators who support using MI must look differently at how lessons are designed and taught and how student achievement is measured and reported to parents.

These changes take their toll, even though they increase student achievement. At a minimum, more time and more energy are required from the faculty. William Bridges (1991), talking about *good* changes in *Managing Transitions* says, "The failure to identify and be ready for the endings and losses that change produces is the largest single problem that organizations in transition encounter" (p. 5). "Adaptability to change," says Warren Bennis (1997), "becomes the most important determinant of survival" (p. 217). Understanding the phases of MI implementation can help staff more quickly adapt and identify necessary changes.

Phases of MI Implementation

Recognizing the phases through which a school—or more specifically, a faculty—will pass doesn't mean that the crooked paths or dead ends can or should be totally avoided. Anticipating and recognizing the phases simply enables planning to take place; realizing that there are some predictable ebbs and flows in the progress toward MI can be reassuring. "Because the stages in an organization's lifecycle are predictable and repetitive, knowing where the organization [is] in the lifecycle enables management to take proactive, preventive measures and deal with future problems earlier or avoid them altogether" (Adizes, 1988, p. xiv). Avoiding problems altogether is not likely; however by anticipating the MI phases through which a school will pass, we can fortify ourselves for a bumpy journey and take steps to smooth the way.

All schools pass through certain sequential phases when implementing MI. The phases, outlined in Figure 7.1, are the same whether you are starting from scratch to build a new school, officially converting an extant school, or gently moving a school to focus more on MI. Variations in context means that some issues will be more significant to some schools than others, but the phases are more alike than different.

Phase 1: Awareness

Awareness is the beginning phase, when there is either a realization that something is lacking in a school or a vision that MI might be a tool to make a good school even better. As educators learn about MI, they often feel that it makes sense because it gives them more tools to use in reaching students.

In some cases, educators recognize how MI would have helped them in their own education. The awareness phase is characterized by

• a recognition that texts and established curriculums are lacking or restrictive,

• a feeling that the status quo is not addressing all students needs, and

• a realization that MI is a way to personalize learning.

The pursuit of MI can be initiated by teachers or administrators; rarely do parents initiate the effort.

Phase 2: Exploration

In the exploration phase, MI is actively investigated, typically by a small group of faculty members (sometimes with parent involvement). The group usually begins by reading and talking about MI and how it might work in their school. Good books for these groups to begin with are *Frames of Mind* (Gardner, 1985) and *Multiple Intelligences In the Classroom* (Armstrong, 1994). The decision to use MI schoolwide has not taken place, so efforts are made to inform other faculty members and garner their support. The exploration phase is characterized by

• lots of reading and talking about MI, sharing of books and articles,

• experimentation with one or two "new" intelligences in selected lessons,

• reactions of excitement (although those teachers not actively involved may respond with "yes, but . . ."), and

• a recognition that it is important to have everyone's support as the pursuit continues.

Questions invariably arise about how MI is different from learning styles, 4-MAT, and other educational practices. Until teachers use MI and experience its success, some are likely to view MI as just another fad.

FIGURE 7.1
The Phases of MI Implementation

PHASE	CHARACTERISTICS	TEACHER BEHAVIORS
1. Awareness	questioning the status quo and dissatisfaction with the "traditional approach" to education; a recognition that there must be a better way to educate students	identifying students who are bored or who are not challenged, allowing lessons to be text driven, eager to find new ways to reach kids
2. Exploration	reading and learning about MI, a nucleus of faculty members meeting regularly to pursue the idea of bringing MI to the school	thinking and talking about how faculty roles and instruction would change from using MI, consciously using a "new" intelligence
3. Courtship	visiting or communicating with schools using MI, generating interest among the rest of the faculty, initial attempts at informing parents and other stakeholders	experimenting with MI, trading ideas and strategies with others, focus on MI in staff development, seeing more students succeed
4. Full-Speed Ahead	most of the faculty begins to use MI, parents understand how MI helps their children, MI is used regularly, signs and graphics throughout the school extol its virtues	assessment and reporting practices begin to change, much enthusiasm as teachers work collaboratively in many different directions
5. Roadblocks	internal or external obstacles are encountered, there are questions about the merits of MI and how it can be used to help students	feelings of frustration or defensiveness can occur, possibility that faculty divides into pro- and anti-MI camps
6. Regrouping	reflection leads to a commitment to MI based on both the gains and costs associated with its use, a realization that using MI doesn't solve all problems	the pace slows, more focus on reflection and refinement of MI practices, a push toward understanding
7. An MI School; An MI Learning Community	MI affects all areas of the school: curriculum, instruction, assessment, relations among faculty and with parents; a recognition that the journey has as much value as the destination	engagement in all aspects of curriculum, pedagogy, and assessment, working as colleagues, a recognition that becoming an MI school will always be a work in progress

Phase 3: Courtship

During the courtship phase, many teachers become comfortable with the tenets of MI theory and its application and begin to use it in their classrooms. Staff clarify what MI entails and discuss the implications for students and faculty. Administrators and teachers agree that MI has the potential to reach more students, and the theory is shared with parents and the larger community. The courtship phase includes

- an evaluation of how present practices would work with a MI approach;
- efforts to look to others for guidance and inspiration (e.g., corresponding and visiting with other schools that are using MI);
- a focus on using MI in instruction, with students responding positively;
- the use of MI at different levels schoolwide (largely depending on teacher enthusiasm); and
- efforts to answer questions from parents and the community about the value of MI.

In this phase, teachers often overuse MI, trying to fit too many intelligences into a particular lesson or even trying to use all the intelligences in every lesson. Teachers feel a real sense of excitement and empowerment, as using MI frees them from textbooks and taps into their creativity. MI is often seen as a goal in itself, rather than as a tool for improving student achievement.

Phase 4: Full-Speed Ahead

At this point, there is general recognition that the school is an "MI School." Faculty members are enthusiastic and parents begin to understand how using MI will help their children. Teachers and administrators begin to explore how using MI can and should affect other parts of their program. The full-speed ahead phase is characterized by

- the regular use of MI by all (or almost all) faculty,
- the acceptance of MI by parents and community,
- high-energy efforts to try to do everything at once,
- increased sharing of ideas among faculty, as working relationships change, and
- an understanding that student assessment and communication with parents must change if MI is to be effective.

Excitement and satisfaction pervade the school. Staff are using MI in a variety of ways and devoting great energy to looking at all aspects of the school. As each innovation and success increases expectations for the future, some teachers begin to wonder when the pace will let up.

Phase 5: Roadblocks

Success has set the stage for some frustration. Crooked roads and dead ends begin to appear as wonderfully creative ideas meet pragmatic realities. Part of the difficulty is that there are so many things that seem to need to be addressed, seemingly all at once. The roadblocks phase is characterized by

- staff changes, either through natural causes (retirement, maternity leave, relocation) or because some teachers desire a more traditional setting;
- a press for traditional accountability as some teachers and parents question the use of MI;
- teacher concerns about what using MI means for curriculum continuity; and
- some faculty dissension, as increased dialogue has highlighted areas where disagreements exist.

The challenges of this phase require particularly strong administrative vision and leadership. Without a strong principal and without strong leadership from within the faculty, the school can devolve into factions that disagree on the merits of MI and how much time its implementation requires. As new staff join the faculty, special attention needs to be given to orientation, training, and support.

Phase 6: Regrouping

A realistic view of both what is possible and how long it will take to accomplish that goal is the result of many dialogues among faculty members. During the phase called regrouping, MI has a powerful influence on thinking and how educational issues are framed, but it is not seen as a panacea. MI is viewed as a tool, rather than a goal. Instead of focusing on creating new ways to use MI, faculty members give more time to evaluating and refining the MI strategies that they are already using. Regrouping is characterized by

- sustained experience with MI, which means that teachers can identify students who have flourished using MI;
- an emphasis on prioritizing and focusing efforts, realizing that everything can't be done at once; and
- efforts to establish support systems and ongoing staff development, as everyone recognizes that faculty members are at different levels in implementing MI.

The highs associated with implementing MI are long gone. The faculty has enough experience with MI to appreciate its benefits and costs. How to maintain the momentum for MI while prioritizing and focusing becomes the challenge for the school leadership.

Phase 7: The MI Learning Community

In this phase, MI is an integral part of the school, transcending individual personalities. It is embraced by educators, students, and parents as a tool that helps identify and nurture student strengths while advancing student growth in traditional academic areas. The learning community phase is characterized by

- more students succeeding;
- the acceptance of MI as a tool for accomplishing educational goals;

- the blending of MI into the school culture (e.g., in faculty discussions, wall and hall decorations, and notes home to parents);
- the use of MI to motivate students to learn and teachers to teach;
- the use of assessment tools and techniques that focus on understanding, not just rote memorization and recitation;
- the use of MI in faculty hiring, teacher evaluation, and staff development efforts; and
- parent and community support for MI and widespread understanding of how its use can help students and teachers grow.

Despite the gains made with MI, a school using MI will always be a work in progress; the *becoming* is never finished! That is, teachers will continue to reflect on how MI is used and search for better ways. Although all schools are works in progress, the pace of change may be faster at an MI school because curriculum and assessment are so teacher-driven. Experience and effort yield success and new ways of using MI to help students learn, but this process will also plant the seeds for higher aspirations. Consequently, given enough time and enough progress, a school that reaches the learning community phase will probably recycle back to roadblocks and travel the last few phases again. Here, too, strong administrative leadership is required to help the faculty balance worthy goals versus pragmatic realities.

My comments about schools passing and moving through phases notwithstanding, the reality is that schools don't move at all. It is the teachers and administrators working together who move through the phases. And given the vagaries of human nature, we all move a bit differently. Dealing with these differences is part of the leadership challenge.

How to Survive and Thrive

The path to MI implementation is not always easy. Yet surviving—indeed, thriving—is possible! We can start by recognizing that there are phases to MI implementation, that the path is not always wide and downhill, and that obstacles and setbacks are inevitable. Beyond that, three factors greatly increase the likelihood that teachers will thrive while wading into MI waters:

1. *The faculty must maintain a commitment to students; they must be doing MI for the right reasons.* Under the best of circumstances, implementing MI requires additional time, energy, and creativity from teachers. Pursuing MI because it is fashionable or because it is mandated almost surely guarantees frustration, if not failure. The right reason—indeed the only reason—to bring MI into the classroom is to enable all students to learn more, to reach their potential. A commitment to students not only ensures that students will be the center of our efforts, as they should be, but it keeps MI in perspective. By focusing on students, we are reminded that MI is a tool, not an end in itself. The bottom line must be "Do students benefit?"

2. *Teachers are far more likely to thrive when they have the support of their peers, when they work and learn as colleagues.* Teaching can be a lonely road, but when teachers make time to bounce ideas off colleagues, revel in their successes, and groan together over their mistakes, the journey is much more pleasant and the energy level higher.

3. *Teachers must have the support of the administration.* In every school setting teachers need administrators who trust and respect them and who understand the pull of the often conflicting responsibilities that adults have in their lives. Administrators need to remember that teacher creativity is tied to trust, and teacher efforts are related to appreciation. It's essential that administrators walk with teachers on the MI journey.

Staff Development

As teachers and administrators pass through the MI phases, the need for faculty development and growth is enormous and ongoing. Staff development activities are important, but they are only a beginning, at least as staff development activities have typically been fashioned. Although there is merit in an outsider sharing experiences for a morning or a day with a faculty, that is only the beginning.

What is far more powerful is to establish a culture that encourages faculty learning. In working with MI, teachers need to do more than learn a new curriculum or a new way to measure student growth. Pursuing MI can become a vehicle for them to learn with and from colleagues, to be part of an enterprise that continually seeks information and reflects on whether there is a better way to meet student needs. Staff development strategies "should explicitly concentrate on the dual goals of implementing a project successfully and influencing the collegial climate of the school as an organization" (Fullan, 1990, p. 12).

At New City, we address staff development needs throughout the year. We begin during August inservice training, which is typically seven days, often including an overnight retreat, and continue on the two inservice training days held during the school year. The work of our faculty committees also pursues staff development needs during the year.

Inservice Training

All of our staff development efforts are valuable, but the August inservice training is especially important because it offers a continuous period for addressing complex issues. Plus, what is done in August helps set the tone for the school year. Despite the luxury of a week to work together before students arrive and the school year officially begins, this time is busy. In addition to getting rooms ready, obtaining supplies, and preparing records, we always focus on various aspects of our MI implementation. What to teach, how to teach it, and how to measure what students have learned (curriculum, pedagogy, and assessment) are always discussed.

Recently we spent three half-days in August on curriculum mapping. We started the process the previous spring by having all grade-level teams identify the skills and concepts they were teaching in social studies. These curriculum maps were shared with the entire faculty as we all looked for gaps and redundancies and then compared our curriculum to sets of social studies standards. After this analysis, we talked in grade-level groups about how MI can be used in our instruction and how we can record and assess students' progress.

We have also used our August inservice training to talk about what should be included in our students' portfolios and how to best use our linguistic and logical-mathematical rubrics. For several years we have spent some time on the concept of genuine understanding (students using skills and information in new and novel ways), and working on how teachers could teach for this goal and how it could be communicated to parents. We have also developed "throughlines" for each grade. Throughlines are "goals which identify the concepts, processes, and skills about which we want students to develop understanding" (Blythe, 1998). We determined how throughlines can be supported by our use of MI. In addition, teachers from adjacent grades always meet and share information about students; on a few occasions we have used students' portfolios as aids. The portfolio discussions invariably lead to reflections on how we use portfolios as well as observations about the individual students.

Although the two inservice training days held during the school year (one in the fall and one in the spring) are isolated, they allow us to reinforce important themes or to address needs identified since August. One year, for example, several teachers from different grades individually expressed concerns about students who were having difficulties. It was clear to me that these teachers shared some common concerns. As a result, I began inservice training by asking teachers to think of the three students in their classrooms who were struggling the most as well as the three students who caused them the most frustration. I then asked teammates, those teaching the same grade level, to see if they had identified the same students. Then I had teachers identify the intelligences in which these students were the strongest and the weakest, looking for patterns. Not surprisingly, at the risk of generalizing, we found that the students who struggle the most are those who are weakest in the scholastic intelligences. Those who are the most frustrating to teachers are those who are the weakest in the personal intelligences. From there, we revisited the role of the nonscholastic intelligences in helping kids learn, though we'd been focusing on those intelligences for years.

Faculty Committees

Faculty committees are the primary engine for our staff development efforts. They operate a bit differently from inservice training because the focus is narrower and the time line longer. We have had committees review our assessment techniques, share ideas about incorporating MI in instruction, map our social studies curriculum (continuing work from our August inservice training), and search for ways to support our valuing of racial and socioeconomic diversity throughout our curriculum. These committees can take credit for creating the format for our progress reports, initiating Intake Conferences and Portfolio Nights, and developing rubrics for the linguistic and logical-mathematical intelligences. When we created the first page of our progress report, which focuses exclusively on the personal intelligences, a faculty committee developed a handbook for new teachers, to help them address these intelligences. While the nature of the focus and activity varies, depending on the committee, in every case faculty members—teachers and administrators working together—are refining efforts and seeking new ways to help students learn. Senge's comment about the learning organization applies:

> Real learning gets at the heart of what it means to be human. Through learning we re-create ourselves. Through learning we re-perceive the world and our relationship to it. Through learning we extend our capacity to create, to be part of the generative process of life (1990, p. 14).

Aspects of the MI Phases

The growth of children through developmental stages is never as clear or steady as we might think. The same holds true for the phases of MI implementation. Depending upon a host of variables—ranging from the quality, open-mindedness, and stability of the faculty to political support and community context—some phases will take far longer to pass through than others. And realistically, some schools may be "stuck" in a phase for a period of time. That's where leadership comes in.

The principal's job is not to make teachers happy. Rather, it is to create a climate in which teachers are supported and challenged, one in which they can learn and grow. If that takes place, students will learn and the teachers will be happy.

The role of the principal is to lead, to work with faculty members to reach consensus, to anticipate the crooked paths and dead ends so they can be avoided or passed through with as little pain and wasted energy as possible. The days of hierarchical bosses who used titles and coercion to mandate change are gone. Particularly in an MI school, a school fueled by teacher creativity and commitment, the leader must be a visionary and a listener. A leader's job is to take you where you weren't sure you wanted to go and to allow and help you be happy once you've arrived. Understanding and recognizing the phases of MI implementation can help leaders do just that.

Faculty Support and Receptivity

Implementing any sort of change always means walking a fine line between what is desired and what is realistic. At New City School we are aware that we often make compromises due to limited financial resources. As a result, when we have ideas, we put them on a list of what we want and then compare the costs to how much we can spend. We establish priorities, which reflect that we cannot afford everything we desire. The process is often painful but we understand financial limitations and make conscious decisions.

Just as often, without realizing it, we walk the same fine line between what is best and what is possible in other areas. This happens when the resources that can be allocated are not dollars but faculty support and receptivity. For example, just as we recognize that the ideal is 1 computer per student, we know that we can afford only 3 computers for 28 students. We also recognize that while it would be ideal for a student's portfolio to contain several examples of each of the multiple intelligences each year, that ideal isn't feasible either. Given our teachers' available time and energy, including a minimum of one item reflecting each intelligence every year is a more realistic goal. In addition, while we believe that it would be best for each student to *routinely* show understanding through projects, exhibitions, and portfolios, our teachers don't have the time and energy to achieve that goal either.

Given that we find ways to do those things that we truly value, the essential resources are teacher support and teacher receptivity. If teachers fully embrace an implementation, the sky is the limit! More can be done than was thought possible and setbacks are seen as minor obstacles to the goal. If teachers do not value the innovation (whether it is MI or some other strategy or technique), the cost of implementation increases, in part because the perceived value is so low. Simply stated, this means that the success of any change effort is a result of the interplay between two variables: the perceived quality of the innovation and its acceptance, determined by teacher support and teacher receptivity. Judging the potential success of an innovation such as MI only on its merit, considering its potential without taking into consideration how it is received by those implementing it, is shortsighted.

For example, the use of portfolios to assess student progress is an idea that has great potential and merit, but just hasn't worked at New City School. Although we use portfolios at every grade level, they are usually a collection of artifacts, that, while interesting, are not useful in recording student growth and progress. Faculty have not committed themselves to using portfolios in a more expansive way: the success of the innovation is hampered by the lack of teacher acceptance. Leaders need to spend considerable energy in the exploration and courtship phases to create enthusiasm and engender support from the faculty. Faculty support creates resources that will be spent during the roadblock phase. Without sufficient resources—faculty enthusiasm and support—the cost is much higher than the gain, and the implementation will run aground.

✦ ✦ ✦

For Faculty Discussion

1. Other than the phases of MI implementation, in what other ways is an organization like an organism? What are the implications of these similarities?
2. Which phase is our school in now?
3. After identifying our school's overall phase of implementation, try to identify where specific components of the school might be. For example, do differences exist in progress on curriculum development, assessment, and reporting to parents? Are particular grades or sections of the school more advanced in their use of MI? If the answer is yes to either of those questions, why is that?
4. Now that we are aware of the phases of MI implementation, what could we be doing differently?

8 | SUPPORTING TEACHER GROWTH WITH LEADERSHIP

When Elizabeth greets the start of summer vacation by saying, "I had a great year. I can't wait until September!" she is really saying, "I had a great teacher!" And when David's mom says, "I love the New City School," she really means "*Every* year at New City has been good for David. He had a wonderful teacher, followed by a superb teacher, and then a great teacher." Each of us can look back on *the* teacher who made a difference for us. We may not remember the formal curriculum or what knowledge or particular set of skills we learned from that teacher, but we know that person made a difference in our lives. Regardless of how old we were or the subject we were studying, we remember how the teacher believed in us, held high expectations for us, understood us, and cared for us. Indeed, in many cases, we chose to become teachers because of the influence of that one teacher.

Clearly, the teacher is the most important factor in a child's education. Good schools are simply buildings filled with good teachers, and great schools are simply buildings filled with great teachers. A rich and challenging curriculum helps teachers become more effective, to be sure. But above all, it is the quality of the teachers that makes the difference for children.

Leadership

All of us—principals, assistant principals, curriculum developers and specialists, teacher leaders, and university faculty—need to do everything that we can to help teachers grow and develop. When teachers use MI, their roles change and professional growth and development become more important. Teachers who work with MI find creative ways to develop curriculum and assessment tools. They focus on helping students use all their strengths to learn how to solve problems and work collaboratively. Rather than working in isolation, these teachers usually work and learn with others.

The MI journey is ongoing. As we move forward we realize that what appears to be the summit is, in fact, just a crest that is followed by another peak beyond the horizon. Gains are almost always accompanied by a desire to do more. The more we know, the more we know what we don't know. The faculty moves forward in using MI and then periodically slows and retrenches. Then momentum builds and the school spurts forward again.

Of course, a school doesn't really "spurt." Rather, the people in the organization take stock of what they have learned, reflecting on what worked and what didn't, and then they try different ways of using MI to help students grow. Constant movement and growth is invigorating and empowering; it is also draining and frustrating. Growth can be only sustained in an environment where teacher growth is valued and supported by strong leadership in both words and action.

Make New Mistakes

We realize that children learn best when they construct knowledge and come to understanding by discovering learning in a meaningful way. In contrast to the traditional hierarchical classroom where the teacher disseminates knowledge, in a constructivist classroom learning is typically messier and often takes longer. Because the student has constructed knowledge, the learning that takes place is richer and in a meaningful context. As a result, what is learned is more likely to be understood and retained. Constructivist classrooms are busy places where students are active experiential learners, testing hypotheses as they seek understanding. Simply put, teaching with a constructivist philosophy means creating situations for students to learn from firsthand experiences, providing opportunities for them to have the "Aha!" experience, when the light of understanding goes on because they have created meaning by *discovering* an important concept or skill.

The process of learning is no different for adults. We also learn best when we are able to construct meaning in finding "Aha!" solutions.

> Individuals bring past experiences and beliefs, as well as their cultural histories and world views, into the process of learning; all of these influence how we interact with and interpret our encounters with new ideas and events. As our personal encounters are mediated with the world, we construct and attribute meaning to these encounters, building new knowledge in the process. This constructive, interpretative work is facilitated and deepened when it is undertaken with others and with reflection.(Lambert, 1995, p. xii).

Just as students better understand how an electrical circuit works if they assemble one (constructing knowledge), rather than just read about it, teachers gain when they construct meaning in their learning. It will be easier, for example, for teachers to understand how students can use their logical-mathematical intelligence to make a Venn diagram to compare stories if they have also done so. Even if administrators think they know the "right" way to use a particular intelligence in the classroom, even if they know the best way to create student portfolios, they still need to create opportunities for their teachers to come to these understandings. We respond better to a guideline than an edict, and that is no less true when we are learning. Perhaps the best way to envision an environment where teachers learn and grow constructively is captured by Esther Dyson's (1998) recommendation to "make new mistakes" (p. 346). That is a profound statement, full of implications for growth and development:

- There is nothing wrong with making a mistake. It is good to take risks and try new things, though you will likely make mistakes in the process.
- As long as the mistakes are new ones, you are learning and growing; make mistakes but learn from them so they are not repeated.
- If teachers are to benefit from making new mistakes, they must be allowed time for reflection.

If teachers are to construct knowledge by creating meaning, they must be able to reflect on their experiences. Facilitate reflection by opening a faculty meeting with this statement: "Take a few minutes to think of something you did this week that didn't work as well as you had hoped. What will you do differently next time?" When doing so, it is always important to point out, as Dyson suggests, that the goal is not to avoid mistakes but rather to learn from them so that they are not repeated.

Making new mistakes is an important part of learning constructively. If we want an environment where teachers can take risks and learn constructively, they must be allowed to make new mistakes.

Almost by definition, constructivist learning implies acceptance of missteps, dead-end roads, and failures. And, when teachers are implementing MI and creating curriculum and developing assessment tools, it is important for an administrator to say that missteps are acceptable, even desirable. What matters most, however, is how an administrator responds to the mistakes. Talking about and endorsing "make new mistakes" is a good start, but actions must follow words.

When I schedule formal observations with my teachers, I sometimes say, "Try something new during this lesson. If it works, great. But if it doesn't, we can talk about what went wrong and how to change things in the future." The expectation is clear: learning, not perfection, is the goal. Because risk taking is not generally part of the educational culture, this message needs to be repeated.

A powerful way for administrators to help teachers take risks and try new things is to publicly share mistakes and errors with the faculty. A litany of my mistakes would turn this book into a multi-volume series, but one example may illustrate my point. At New City, the annual goal-setting process begins in the fall when teachers are asked to generate their professional goals. After drafting the goals, each teacher meets with an administrator to talk about the appropriateness of the goals and how progress will be measured. During the year, my assistants and I use observations, dialogue, and memos to check with teachers on how they are addressing their goals. At the end of each year, we review and discuss the goals with the teachers. We typically asked teachers to focus on one, two, or three goals.

A few years ago, I decided that we needed to ask each teacher to set five professional goals for the year. Teachers were asked to generate one goal to show how they would address each of the three points in our New City mission statement: academics, ambience, and diversity. In addition, teachers would be asked to generate a goal for using MI and one for displaying collegiality. My assistants cautioned me that it was not realistic to have so many goals, but I persevered. "All of these are important," I argued. "How can we do any less?" (As you have probably already guessed, I confused what was desirable with what was feasible.)

No sooner had the memo gone to teachers than the discussion began. Five was definitely too many goals! As the year progressed and dialogue continued, it became clearer that this ambitious approach simply wasn't feasible. Thinking about five goals caused many teachers to diffuse their efforts. In mid-January I shared the realization that five goals was too many and apologized for being unrealistic. Subsequently, each time we met with teachers about the progress they were making toward their goals, I made a point of noting that five was an unrealistic number and asked "What should we *really* focus on?" (Because everyone had already generated five goals and begun to work toward them, deleting some goals in the middle of the year didn't seem like a good idea.) The following year I made a point, again, of taking responsibility for the previous year's error. This time we asked teachers to generate one professional goal for technology along with a team goal, generated in collaboration with their teammates. (All members of the teaching team must agree to the same team goal, one that focuses on their working relationships and ability to work as a team.)

The point is a simple but powerful one: actions speak louder than words. As William Bridges (1991), author of *Managing Transitions*, says, "Leaders send many more messages than they realize or intend to. Unless the leader is modeling the behavior that he or she is seeking to develop in others, things aren't likely to change very much" (p. 14). The teachers knew that I was trying new strategies and that I wasn't always successful either. They could see that I was making new mistakes. Teachers must know that we will support them in their successes and their failures.

What You Measure Is What You Value

The relationship between measurement and value holds true for students (see Chapter 4), and adults. All of us work to do well on the issues on which we will be evaluated. If there is a disparity between what is said to be important and what is actually measured, we respond to what is measured.

Years and schools ago, when I first became a principal, I was told that I had two priorities: student academic achievement and teacher development. Academics were the highest priority and I would be evaluated on how well my students performed on standardized tests. Strong staff supervision was also essential and this, too, would factor into how I would be judged. (I didn't necessarily agree with the emphasis on standardized tests but as long as I knew the rules, I figured that I would be OK.)

Imagine my surprise, then, when for the first three months of school, the topic most discussed by the district supervisors in the central office seemed to be whether any parents complained to them. If a parent called the district to complain or even to ask a question, the principal of that child's school heard about it quickly, loudly, and often. If no one called or wrote to express unhappiness, the principal was presumably doing a good job. If there was an upset parent, even one, the principal was doing something wrong. Beyond parent concerns, all the central office staff ever asked me about was whether my reports and forms were going to be turned in on time. There was no discussion of teacher development and little time was spent on student achievement.

I also recall that each principal had to produce a lengthy school-based action plan based on the district's objectives. Once the action plan was submitted, however, little attention was given to it. In fact, it seemed that the timeliness of the report was more important than its contents. Principals shared tips about where and how to have the documents quickly copied, but not what might be written on the pages. Similarly, despite the rhetoric about my focusing on teacher supervision, no one from the central office asked me how often—or even if—I was observing teachers. Yet principals were required to give every teacher a written evaluation in February. By the end of February all of the evaluations were written, signed by the teachers and me, and submitted to the central office before any of my supervisors bothered to look at what I had written. And while standardized test scores were important—they occupied almost all of the dialogue in the district during the spring—it was clear to me that the supervisors viewed late reports and complaints from parents as their most serious concerns.

Consequently, as I look back upon my experience, keeping parents' complaints to a minimum and submitting reports in a timely manner became a major focus of my efforts. In fact, our students did achieve and our teachers did grow, but they did so almost in spite of the central office, not because the staff actively supported them. The actions of the superintendent and the deputies spoke far louder than their words about what was really valued.

In MI schools, teachers need to know that the focus is on providing opportunities for students to use all of the intelligences in the classroom. How this understanding is communicated—whether it emanates from a professional goal, as described above, or is simply discussed in faculty meetings or sought in observations—is less important than ensuring that teachers know what the school values and what they will be evaluated on. If, for example, teachers know that their evaluations will be based, in part, on how well they incorporate the multiple intelligences in their classrooms, they will work more diligently to ensure that this takes place. I am not suggesting that implementing MI should be the only criterion on which teachers are evaluated. If using MI is valued, however, this needs to be reflected in the messages given to teachers.

The Principal's Job

All of us like to be liked and all of us want to work in an environment where congeniality (distinct from collegiality) is the norm. The principal is in a unique position, controlling scarce resources and offering both official approval and sanction, to affect how people feel about where they work. Thus it is easy to fall prey to the idea that the principal's job is to make teachers happy, and that a happy faculty means a good school. Presumably, a happy teacher performs better than an unhappy teacher. But focusing on making everyone happy is an invitation to disaster.

Inevitably, running a school involves making choices, decisions that will likely leave someone unhappy. The times when a decision is a win-win for all, when everyone is in agreement and supportive are too rare. The frequency of win-win decisions can be increased by soliciting input from the relevant individuals, taking all of the variables into consideration, and making fair and consistent decisions. Even then, however, a degree of conflict is inevitable. Whether allocating scarce resources or making personnel decisions, the principal will make some people unhappy. Happiness cannot be the goal; it must be a by-product. The principal's job is to create an environment where children and adults learn and grow. If teachers are growing and learning, their chances of being happy will increase.

Inherent in the quest for the new, of course, is a rejection of the old. And so begins the process of making choices that often sets one camp against another. Advocates of the old way of teaching can feel criticized and rejected, especially if extra resources—including time and attention—are given to teachers who are pursuing MI. Making choices doesn't mean being insensitive to people's feelings.

A principal can—and should—appreciate the different ways teachers approach curriculum and instruction, respect individuality, and be cognizant of the different stages teachers are at in their personal lives. Nevertheless, the principal's job is to take a stand and make decisions based on what is good for the students.

Although not every solution will make everyone happy, some conflicts can be avoided or ameliorated by soliciting opinions in a way that brings people on board. Decisions made in isolation, even informed or good decisions, are not as strong as those that have been discussed with others. Discussions must be conducted in a way that lets teachers know they are being asked to contribute ideas, not make a decision. Seeking ideas from the staff not only generally improves the quality of the decision, it almost always increases its acceptability.

Perhaps the most difficult decision a principal must make is when to let a bad teacher go. We should not allow poor teachers to remain in our schools. We wouldn't go to a mediocre dentist or to a car mechanic who was barely adequate, so why should we ask parents to trust their children to teachers who continue to perform less than adequately? Almost all educators would agree with this statement, yet whenever someone is dismissed or a contract is not renewed, many faculty members seem to close ranks and identify with the teacher who was let go, even if they complained about the individual the previous week!

To some degree this sort of unquestioning support comes from normal human compassion and empathy, but it is also endemic in a profession in which such actions are all too rare. The seeming subjectivity of the teacher evaluation process, reinforced by the need for confidentiality to protect both the employee's and employer's rights, means that much of the information on which decisions are made must be unknown to the public. Privacy has the potential to create professional paranoia among the faculty. Despite how well they perform, their positive relationship with the principal, or their tenure status, some teachers are prone to ask "Am I next?" The happiness scale in any school drops when hard decisions are made, even when they affect the worst teachers in the building.

Regardless of how clear and easy these kinds of decisions are in the abstract, they are hard decisions to make and stand by. And having made one such decision, it is even harder to make another, knowing what is ahead. If a principal is guided by happiness as a goal, decisions are made based on what is easy and what is least likely to upset the organizational applecart. Although such decisions may make life easier for many, the students lose. By focusing on creating an environment where everyone grows, students and teachers will be successful and happiness will come.

Perception Is Reality

All of us act on our perceptions; we respond to the reality that we define and see. That should be obvious. What is less obvious to many of us, however, is that others' perceptions are not the same as ours. All too often these differences, sometimes very logically based differences, do not surface until they are part of a disagreement. By then, what started as small misunderstandings or predictable differences have become entrenched positions and major conflicts.

This is not to suggest that people should not hold different perceptions or that the goal should be for everyone to see everything the same way. There is a special richness that comes from the understanding and consensus derived from an exchange of disparate opinions. Whatever the outcome or product that is fashioned, it will be stronger if the process took into consideration a variety of perceptions.

Sometimes the different perceptions are obvious from the beginning, as when people have opposing values or beliefs. Even people who share the same basic educational philosophy may have radically different perceptions. There are many reasons why this is so. In part, our background and culture influence how we view situations and what opinions we hold on issues. Surfacing these differences and finding common ground is a much stronger approach than pretending that they do not exist. As society and our work environments become more racially, ethnically, culturally, and socioeconomically diverse, we must learn to anticipate differences and handle them in a positive manner.

We should also expect people to look differently at issues as a result of the job they hold. While teachers and principals all want students to succeed, they are likely to have different opinions about the need of the principal to play the role of a strong school disciplinarian or the need for teachers to submit weekly lesson plans. Teachers may want the former and principals the latter!

Years ago, when I was teaching, I remember dreading December because I knew that my class would need an inordinately large amount of preparation for their role in the evening holiday show. Sure, the kids enjoyed it and parents looked forward to the evening, but I felt as if the preparation was detracting from time I wanted to spend more productively, focusing on the 3 Rs. As a result, I did what was necessary and no more. (It embarrasses me to admit that I did not then see how the holiday show could play into my students' strengths and help them grow. My only defense is that this was long before the concept of MI was recognized!)

Then I became a principal in another school district. I remember eagerly looking forward to the holiday program. I saw it as a positive way to bring parents into the school. But the faculty was far less enthusiastic! Their attitude puzzled me and for a nanosecond I wondered, "Why don't these teachers understand?" Then it dawned on me that I had held exactly that view a couple years earlier. Each position has some merit in this example; each was a function of the occupational roles people play, which powerfully influence how they perceive the same situation.

Similarly, my ill-fated attempt to introduce the MI Profile (see Chapter 7) manifested this same dilemma at New City School. In the minds of teachers, they were going to be asked to identify a student's level of proficiency in each of the intelligences. They naturally felt accountable, even for—especially for—the intelligences in which they held little or no expertise. In my mind, using the MI Profile was a way to help teachers use the intelligences and monitor student progress. Because I was not holding conferences with parents, I did not feel the same level of accountability—and vulnerability—that the teachers did.

People act on their perceptions; thus, it is important that perceptions be shared. Otherwise, we too easily assume that everyone is on the same page—until things go awry and communication breaks down. Once people stop communicating, distrust grows and people begin to attribute negative motives to one another. At best, inefficiency results. At worst, communication breaks down and relationships dissolve. People see those who do not share their views as adversaries.

What can be done? It is important to legitimize the natural and appropriate differences and perceptions that exist by creating an environment where all opinions are valued and respected. I have found the extensive use of surveys to be helpful in this process. I periodically survey faculty members and parents to see how they view certain issues. The data from the surveys serve as my reality check, allowing me to see how others perceive issues. New City parents are sent surveys (through the mail with a stamped, self-addressed envelope enclosed) when they first enroll their children at New City and again each spring. An example of the spring parent survey is shown in Appendix D. At times I have sent surveys that focus on particular issues or

events (e.g., after parent-teacher conferences, Portfolio Night, and our progress report).

I periodically survey the faculty to ask for their opinions and perceptions. Each spring I ask them to give feedback to me and my assistants, letting us know how we are doing our jobs. Here again, it is important that I know their perceptions of the school and our performance. Although it isn't always easy to hear what is said, it is important that I listen.

Finally, my favorite example of how perceptions differ—in this case how we see ourselves as radically different from how others see us (and reality)—comes from *In Search of Excellence* (Peters & Waterman Jr., 1982):

> In a recent psychological study, when a random sample of male adults were asked to rank themselves on "the ability to get along with others," all subjects, 100%, put themselves in the top one-half of the population. Sixty percent put themselves in the top 10% of the population, and a full 25% ever so humbly thought that they were in the top 1% of the population.
>
> In a parallel finding, 70% rated themselves in the top quartile, top one-fourth, in leadership; only 2% felt that they were below-average as leaders.
>
> Finally, in an area where self-deception should be hard, for most males at least, 60% said that they were in the top quartile, top one-fourth, in athletic ability; only 6% said they were below average.

Until I read that, I had thought I was athletic.

Your Decisions, My Decisions, Our Decisions

More and more we learn that teams are more productive than individuals, that collaboration is the name of the game. Today every manager worth her salt believes that employees should be empowered, knows that decision making is best when it is shared, and understands that a productive work setting is one where ideas are solicited from all levels of the hierarchy. These guiding principles are no less true in schools.

In schools that value collaboration, teachers are more likely to feel a sense of ownership about their jobs. They offer suggestions and try to become part of the solution. That is the good news. The bad news is that this kind of employee involvement and empowerment carries with it a potential unanticipated cost. Unless it is done carefully, including teachers in the decision-making process can cause major rifts between teachers and principals. And often it is the "best" principals, those who are the most inclusive and value this kind of teacher involvement, who have the most difficulties.

Realistically, despite the flattening of the hierarchy for certain decisions and procedures, some issues remain the responsibility of the principal (or other administrator). Certainly hiring and firing decisions fall here; so, too, do some budgetary decisions and many decisions about parent relationships. These will vary by school, of course, but what will not vary is that some decisions must remain with the principals.

As a result, unless managers—in this case, principals—are very clear about who has what responsibility for which decisions, and unless they make that distinction known to everyone involved—in this case, teachers—they are likely to have difficulties with teachers who feel that they were not heard simply because they did not get what they wanted. The distinction between making suggestions and having responsibility for making decisions can be fuzzy in the best of situations. It is easy for someone whose opinion is solicited to feel that she is being asked to make the decision. As management reaches out to include more employees in the circle of who's heard, teachers who have previously not exercised judgment on areas outside of their locus of control are now being asked their opinions about schoolwide procedures and policies. Teachers who haven't been part of the decision-making process may believe that they are being asked to make the decision when, in fact, they are being asked to provide suggestions to the decision makers who will ultimately make the decision. Because teachers deal directly with students and their parents, the focus of the school's efforts, this confusion of roles is exacerbated and teachers are likely to feel that their opinions are the right decisions.

Given that ideas from teachers are essential to school improvement efforts, determining how to empower teachers and solicit their opinions without creating misunderstandings and hard feelings is important. At first glance this task might seem easy, after all, principals simply need to make clear the distinctions between making suggestions and making decisions. The difficulty lies in doing so without damaging relations with the staff.

Inevitably, the principal wants teachers to feel that they are equal partners at the decision-making table, especially in an MI school where success depends on all faculty members working together as colleagues. But having invited the teachers to share their opinions and letting them know that they are important members of the process, it can be difficult for the principal to remind them that "the suggestions are yours; the decision is mine." Principals are likely to feel that this kind of reminder is counterproductive to the teachers' feeling of worth and empowerment, no matter how well it is said.

As a consequence, principals are likely to gloss over the fact that they are requesting suggestions only and fail to note that the decision remains theirs. Consciously or subconsciously, they want the teachers to feel that everyone stands together, more or less, as equal members of the decision-making process. This tendency is reinforced when the principal feels that the teachers will give her the suggestions she wants, giving her license to make the same decision that she would have made by herself.

Too often the principal asks for ideas or requests comments, feeling confident that teachers see things as she does. Having earlier failed to distinguish between offering suggestions and having responsibility, she listens and nods appropriately as the teachers share their perceptions. If, in fact, the teachers and principal do see things the same, she does not see it as important or necessary to point out who owns the authority for making the decision. Although the responsibility for the decision was hers, she can seemingly share her authority with the teachers because they are in agreement.

That is not always the case. Sometimes it becomes clear that teachers are seeing things differently than the principal, who nonetheless continues to listen quietly. Her purpose is to be sure they have the opportunity to contribute ideas, and she is doing that. She thinks there is no reason to disagree or point out areas where perceptions differ. "It is too bad that they see things differently," she thinks to herself, "but I've asked for their ideas, and now that I have them, I will consider all the information and make my decision."

The principal thinks that she has done what was expected and been a collaborative team member. She asked for ideas, she listened, she considered, and she decided; after all, the responsibility for making the decision is hers. But the teachers will see things differently when they learn that her decision runs counter to the suggestions they provided. They will feel that they were asked for their opinions and then were ignored. Worse, they will feel that they were made to feel part of the decision-making process, but were used as part of a charade. "The principal doesn't care what we think," a teacher may say. "She just asks our opinions so she can say she did so, and then do whatever she wants."

Although there is always a danger of employees feeling ignored or disenfranchised when their recommendations are not followed, the potential increases when principals do not clearly explain what they are—and are not—asking of the teachers and why they are asking it. When asking for the opinions of employees, managers also have a responsibility to help the employees understand who has the decision-making authority and why suggestions from others are being sought.

The phrase "your decisions, my decisions, our decisions," can be a useful tool for helping employees at all levels of the organization understand the difference between offering suggestions and having responsibility. It can serve as a shorthand way of reminding everyone of the need to be clear about who holds the decision-making responsibilities in a situation before opinions are sought and the decision is made. Before requesting recommendations on a particular issue, and on a few occasions throughout the year, school leaders need to make clear the difference between providing feedback and making decisions.

All employees need to understand that there are several kinds of decision-making responsibilities in any organization:

• *Your Decisions* are those that individual employees or work groups can make on their own; they are the decisions delegated to them by management and for which they have responsibility and accountability. How rooms are set up or decorated, how lessons are taught, and dealings with individual students fall here. In an MI school, teachers have even more latitude regarding these decisions. At New City, which yearlong themes are chosen and how intelligences are incorporated into instruction are good examples of "your decisions."

• *My decisions* are the decisions of the principal alone (or the principal and her leadership team); the principal may—in most cases, should—solicit feedback, but making the actual decision and the responsibility for it reside with her. Personnel decisions and some budget decisions are definitely administrative responsibilities. So, too, are many decisions that focus on communication with parents about student progress; in MI schools, such a decision might be deciding whether to administer standardized tests. As another example, a few years ago I refused to acquiesce to strong faculty sentiment that all the narrative pages on our report card (progress report) be condensed and placed in one area. I had talked to enough parents to know that this change would be viewed very negatively, as a diminished commitment to giving students individual attention and respecting all of the intelligences (even though this was not the motivation or sentiment of the faculty).

• *Our decisions* are joint decisions; they are decisions the principal and teachers reach together, through consensus, and for which responsibility is shared. In MI schools, how the intelligences are addressed schoolwide, whether there is a Flow Room, and how students are evaluated regarding the intelligences would fall here. The decision not to use the MI Profile was "our decision" at New City.

The potential for conflict and dissension is ripe when decision-making boundaries are unclear. Despite the many benefits of including teachers in the decision-making process, unless both teachers and principals are clear about when teachers are offering suggestions and when they have responsibility for decisions, much confusion and distrust can be created. The situation is particularly dangerous when principals wrongly assume that teachers share their perceptions. Given the difference in roles and responsibilities, few teachers—even the best ones—are likely to have the global view that the principal does. Similarly, few principals will have a teacher's perspective from the classroom and students' point of view. These differences are both logical and appropriate, but this doesn't diminish the potential for conflict. On the other hand, principals who understand this tension can avoid ill will by making the parameters clear as they ask for recommendations, being clear about where the ultimate decision rests.

◆ ◆ ◆

For Faculty Discussion

1. Ask teachers to think of the teacher who made a difference in their life and to write the person's initials. Then ask, "What did that person do to make such an impression on you?" After giving everyone a minute or two to think about this question, have small groups discuss the characteristics of these special teachers.

2. Share a time when you have made a mistake and learned from it, not repeating the error and moving ahead.

3. On what *formal* criteria are teachers evaluated in your school? On what *informal* criteria are teachers evaluated?

4. Discuss issues on which teachers and principals should view things differently due to the different positions they occupy in the organization. What could be done to minimize the potential for conflict?

Steps to Implement MI

Just as each school is different, so is each MI journey. There are however, some steps that may be helpful in any pursuit of MI.

1. Teachers and administrators—either the entire faculty or a committee—should talk about risk taking. What can be done to help people make *new* mistakes?

2. At least one of teachers' annual goals should include some aspect of MI implementation. It might be as generic as using more MI in the classroom or as specific as focusing on the teacher and her students developing a particular intelligence or two.

3. Administrators should share the "your decision, my decision, our decision" model with the faculty, looking at previous decisions and identifying the appropriate category. (If this seems very hard to do, the administrator might begin the dialogue with a group of seasoned teachers, those with whom she is more comfortable discussing such issues.)

9 | WHAT'S NEXT? THE FUTURE OF MI

Speculating about the future of MI in schools is precarious at best. In 1980, who could have accurately guessed what role technology would play in many schools today? After all, just 20 years ago personal computers were virtually unheard of. I remember buying state-of-the-art Commodore 16K PET computers for New City School in 1982. We were amazed at their power; today my 5-year-old wristwatch has more memory than those computers. Who would have projected such advances in technology? Indeed, projecting into the future in any arena is difficult; that is what makes a pennant race interesting and the stock market nerve-racking!

Looking into the future in education is challenging because, whether we like it or not (and we probably don't), educators often play reactionary roles. That is, we react to pushes and pulls from other sectors of society. Presidents, governors, or commissioners hold press conferences deploring low levels of student achievement, and schools scramble to react. New laws create competition among schools, or increase graduation requirements, or mandate a certain kind of test, and educators develop programs to respond. Lay people run for school board by proclaiming that they are for this or against that and once elected, they begin to influence policies and practices. These kinds of initiatives—pushing for a certain curriculum, longer school year, or higher test scores—aren't necessarily

pernicious; they do, however, mean that the goals and means of schooling are often initiated by noneducators and come to us enmeshed in political battles. Looking ahead at how schooling might change and thinking about how MI might fit into the future effectively means looking at how society might change.

That society *will* change is beyond doubt. In *Leading At the Edge of Chaos* (1998), Daryl Conner says, "Regardless of how ready people are to face it, more change is moving toward us at greater speed and with more complicated implications than we have ever seen" (p. ix). Predictions are always tenuous because there are no guarantees. That caveat aside, however, there *are* some things that we can predict, changes that will affect schools and the use of MI:

• *Continued technological advances will be the norm.* The power of computers will continue to increase while their cost decreases. More uses will be found for technology, from using GPS (Global Positioning Satellites) in farming equipment and rental cars to the development of jogging shoes with computer chips that monitor speed, length of stride, and body weight to adjust the cushion in the soles. How we communicate and access information will change, too. More than 500 million e-mail messages are sent each day, for example, and a collection of every issue of *National Geographic* on CD-ROM fits in a container the size of a shoe box! Sooner than we can imagine, a computer—or computer equivalent— will be on almost every student's desk. What we don't know are the many ways they will be used.

• *Racial, ethnic, and cultural diversity will increase.* Projections based on immigration policies and birth rates indicate that by the year 2050 there will be more racial "minorities" than "majorities" (Caucasians) living in the United States; the present racial majority will become the minority. Neighborhoods and workplaces are becoming increasingly diverse. Although most of our parents lived and worked with people of the same race and background, our students are more likely to live and work with people of different races, cultures, and ethnic backgrounds. Diversity means that the ability to understand and work with others, especially others who are different from us, is an essential skill.

• *The free market, consumer-driven model will become more pervasive in many organizations, including schools.* The deregulation of businesses that began in the 1980s is beginning to affect how education is delivered to "customers" (parents and students). As in other businesses and industries, more energy will go into advertising and marketing, in this case providing information about the relative quality of educational programs. Information will enable parents to make decisions about how schools are organized and, indeed, which schools they wish their children to attend.

We already see evidence of the free market in education. Pick up any educational journal or newspaper and you're likely to see an article about charter schools, voucher plans, or some other form of site-based management in which decisions are made at the school level and parents have a role in governance. While these approaches differ, what they share is placing more decision-making power about the schools children attend in the hands of their parents.

How we respond to change determines whether the change is positive. Given the inevitability of change, it is incumbent that we be as proactive as possible and anticipate how it affects us. Considering all of these changes—in technology, in demographics, and in increased expectations from parents and the community—it is even more important that we develop *students* who know how to

– identify problems,
– use their intelligences to solve problems and create products,
– demonstrate their understanding in a variety of ways, and
– work with others, including people who are both similar to and different from themselves.

And as we face increasing and new forms of competition from charters, vouchers, and home schools, it is even more important that *educators*

– personalize education and work to individualize instruction;
– enable students to develop and use their areas of strength;
– view students' parents as partners and educate them, too;
– offer an environment that supports faculty collegiality and growth; and
– are able to demonstrate that students are prepared for the future.

The good news is that using MI supports educators and students as they strive for these goals. That is not to say that only MI schools can address these needs and prepare students for the future; obviously there are many different high-quality ways to design curriculum and organize instruction. Given the assumptions of MI theory, however, its use increases the likelihood that each student's needs and abilities are recognized and met in a pragmatic way.

In MI schools, children are offered different

ways to learn prescribed curriculum and meet academic goals. In MI schools, a focus is placed on both understanding the problem and understanding oneself. In MI schools, the faculty works and learns together. No, we cannot be sure what the future will hold. I do believe, however, that students in schools that embrace MI have a better chance to succeed in the world of the future because they are developing lifelong learning skills.

The Evolution of MI

In a variety of countries, cultures, and contexts, teachers and administrators see MI as a way to increase their students' chances for success. A little over 15 years after the initial publication of *Frames of Mind*, hundreds of thousands of copies have been sold. But that is only the beginning.

A cottage industry of MI practitioners and products now exists. Scores of books and videos about MI and its implementation are available. Type "multiple intelligences" on a search engine and the results will be thousands of references. Nearly every educational conference features one or more presentations about MI. As one example close to home, the New City School has sponsored three MI conferences and all three have been sold out months in advance. More than 45,000 copies of our faculty's MI books have been sold, and they have been adapted for sales in Australia, New Zealand, and South America. In my position as coordinator of the ASCD Multiple Intelligences Network, each year I hear from hundreds of educators from across the country and around the world, in varying stages of MI implementation.

There is every reason to believe momentum will continue building for MI. Helping students use all of their intelligences to learn agreed-upon skills and attain state, district, and school goals makes a great deal of sense. Indeed, the MI picture is a rosy one.

But as the use of MI in education continues, it will evolve. How MI is used in 2009 will be quite different from how it is used in 1999. Evolution happens with every innovation, but it is even more striking when practitioners have as much latitude as they do with MI. In thinking about the future, I have tried to identify areas where natural evolutions and logical steps will take place.

Assessment, Genuine Understanding, and MI

When used properly, MI widens the lens that we use to look at students. We see them as more than children whose intellect can be measured with a paper and pencil test. Instead, we recognize students who possess many different intelligences, who have different arrays of strengths, and who use these strengths to learn and show what they understand.

There will always be a place for standardized tests, but the use of authentic assessments and portfolios will increase. Students who create projects or present exhibitions can show that their understanding goes beyond rote recall, and in doing so they can capitalize on their stronger intelligences. This "performance perspective" approach to assessment is captured by Blythe: "understanding is a matter of being able to do a variety of thought-provoking things with a topic, such as explaining, finding evidence and examples, generalizing, applying, analogizing, and representing the topic in new ways" (1998, p. 12). Students who can draw from all of their intelligences are more likely to find ways to demonstrate their understanding. As more authentic assessment and performance assessments are used, the line between assessment and instruction becomes blurred because good assessment *is* an integral part of instruction and good instruction *is* an integral part of assessment.

Grant Wiggins'(1998) recommendation to use "backward design" in instructional planning supports the idea of blending assessment and instruction. Rather than beginning planning by focusing on what is to be covered, Wiggins says that we need to begin by determining what students need to know *and how it can be measured*. In other words, how will we know what they know? Once we know our desired end, then we can work backward to plan the actual lesson or unit. This kind of evaluative thinking leads to student performances using a variety of intelligences. These performances are measures of what students know and don't just force students' understanding through a linguistic filter by relying on oral or written responses.

Portfolios support the use of MI and vice versa. Over time teachers will move from viewing portfolios as simple collections of student work to recognizing how they can be used to monitor student progress and development. Portfolios play an important role in helping develop the intrapersonal intelligence because students learn to understand themselves from reviewing their portfolios. And, as we look to the future, technology will reshape what we incorporate into portfolios—digital cameras and scanners will allow us to capture nearly every kind of student performance.

I would be remiss if I did not again caution against the seemingly inevitable desire, once having embraced the concept of MI, to measure and label students in each of the intelligences. If measuring skill or acumen in the intelligences has a purpose and results in teachers understanding the best ways to reach students, then it is worthwhile. But measurement for measurement's sake, with no practical utility, serves no good purpose and may, in fact, be harmful. At a minimum, it wastes time and resources with no appreciable benefit.

Community Partnerships and MI

The emphasis on students demonstrating what they have learned by presenting their projects, exhibitions, and portfolios to various audiences may result in schools working more closely with the community. It makes sense to invite parents and members of the community to see these performances of understanding. This not only raises the bar a bit for students, encouraging them to do their best in preparing for an unknown audience, it also enables those who do not have children in the schools to appreciate what students are learning. Working with the community becomes even more important as accountability in schools becomes an issue. Schools can work more closely with the community through apprenticeships, which are a great way for students, particularly older ones, to learn skills and understand expectations. After all, the ultimate performance of understanding is an authentic one in which the judges are people who work in the field. Everyone benefits when students take classes while also working side by side with architects, musicians, park rangers, graphic designers, lab technicians, and physicians' assistants.

Adult Learning and MI

There is no reason to limit the use of MI to elementary and secondary schools. Many colleges and universities offer courses about how to teach using MI, and at least one institution takes an MI approach in teaching its students. Under the leadership of Greg Miller, the University of Rio Grande (in Rio Grande, Ohio) offers a master's program designed for teachers, museum educators, and others who wish to use an interdisciplinary approach to teaching. The program's core courses, one half of the program, emphasize using MI in teaching, and the rest of the courses have a Fine Arts concentration. Students experience a variety of art, music, dance, and theater courses with an emphasis on how the process of engaging in and appreciating the various forms of art helps them learn. Nationally recognized artists visit the program, and students take a weeklong trip "to the arts" by visiting cultural centers in London, New York, Madrid, Paris, or Rome (at the students' expense). While in these cities, students attend concerts and the theater, go to jazz clubs, and visit museums.

Over time, as universities begin to enroll

students who used all intelligences in learning in elementary and secondary schools, it is only logical that they will continue to use MI as a strategy in their university studies. As in many secondary schools, however, the discipline-based orientation of many faculty members may slow the use of MI in post-secondary education.

Learning Disabilities and MI

As the use of MI becomes more commonplace in schools, children who found only frustration will begin to experience success. We will see that although the term "learning disabled" is applied to students, sometimes it is really the school that has the difficulties. As Thomas Armstrong (1994) points out, when schools offer only one way for students to learn, it is the school that is learning disabled (although the students pay the price). Too often educators have been more concerned with creating narrow academic hierarchies than meeting students' needs. Sadly, as Joe McDonald says in *Redesigning School* (1996), "throughout the twentieth century, we have asked [students] to be academic because we intended to sort them on the basis of their response" (p. 11).

While the range and degree of learning disabilities is wide, the use of MI can help many youngsters who have been labeled "learning disabled" find success. To begin with, an MI approach is student-centered, rather than curriculum-centered. Using tactile methods to help students learn and allowing students to show their understanding by using their spatial, artistic, or bodily-kinesthetic intelligences are strategies that teachers who work with these youngsters have found helpful. For example, students can learn spelling words by manipulating cut-out letters in addition to hearing and saying sounds, by rapping sounds to correspond to letters as they are spelled, or by drawing letters in sand. Unfortunately, the classes in which students design and build rockets, dissect frogs, fashion clay to

capture emotion, or choreograph dance are often limited to the "gifted" students, those who have scored above an arbitrary level on a standardized intelligence test. Yet it is often the "learning disabled" students, those who are not strong in the scholastic intelligences, who would benefit most from these kinds of experiences.

The congruence between using MI and meeting the needs of students who learn differently is a good one: teachers who use MI must understand how their students learn and, knowing that, tailor curriculum and instruction. All children benefit from this approach and attitude, but perhaps none more than the student who encounters difficulties when trying to learn primarily through the linguistic and logical-mathematical intelligences. Traditionally these students' motivation and love of learning become casualties in a setting where their intelligences are not valued.

Using MI is not a panacea for students who have difficulty learning. Some successes will occur when an MI approach is used with students who have difficulties. But simply using MI does not resolve learning disabilities or negate the need for teachers to delve more deeply into their students' understanding. Sally Grimes, of the Cape Code Education Center, says, "MI approaches are often enthusiastically embraced by these [learning disabled] students for they address some of the critical learning issues and open the doors to learning for them. However, the success only scratches the surface in the case of the truly learning disabled because the teacher lacks an in-depth understanding of why the methods are working for the student, how best to maximize such methods, and the intensity and duration of certain aspects that are needed in some instances."

A related concern is that as MI is used successfully to help students with learning disabilities, it may become viewed primarily as a tool for students who are having difficulties. Although the use of MI implies neither a lack of rigor nor a backing away from high academic standards, those who do not understand MI may not accept the idea that MI gives students different tools to learn. The creativity found in an MI approach and students' increased opportunities for success may cause some people to want to see MI as only benefitting those who have difficulty learning. Parent education about MI (described more fully in Chapter 2) is an integral part of implementing MI and preventing such misconceptions.

The Arts and MI

By definition, believing in MI means valuing the arts. After all, an MI approach places the musical, spatial, and bodily-kinesthetic intelligences on a par with the linguistic and logical-mathematical intelligences. As MI gains acceptance and is used more routinely, we should see fewer distinctions between those classrooms where the arts are valued and those where the arts are viewed as an extra. Most teachers will not have as high a level of knowledge or skill in these intelligences as the music, art, and physical education teachers, but they can still ensure the presence of these intelligences in their classrooms and encourage students to use them to learn and show what they understand. At an MI school, balanced budgets aren't achieved by sacrificing the arts. When schools sacrifice the arts, they really are telling many students that how they learn isn't very important.

Valuing and emphasizing the arts will make a difference for students. At New City, I don't expect that this will lead to more of our students becoming adults who make their living as artists, though that is certainly possible. I do expect that our students will continue to value the arts for the rest of their lives. As a result, I am confident that when compared with students who did not attend an MI school, more of our students will pursue art as an avocation and spend many hours painting landscapes, playing the clarinet, or creating pottery in the basement. I am sure that more of our students will visit museums and galleries, attend symphonies and dramatic presentations, and go to dance concerts. In short, they will enjoy life more. If MI had no other effect—and clearly it does—this, alone, would be a good argument for its use.

We need to recognize that the arts play an important role in our society. They tell stories, they capture and communicate emotions, and, as this book recounts, they can be used as tools for learning. But none of these is more significant than the pleasure the arts can give us. Alone among the species on this planet, we have the ability to create and enjoy art; infusing the arts into education, using the arts, helps all of us tap into our human potential.

The Personal Intelligences and MI

As noted in Chapter 6, I believe that one of the most significant contributions of MI theory is the identification and prominence that it gives to the *two* personal intelligences. By defining "people skills" as intrapersonal and interpersonal intelligences—knowledge of self and understanding of others—Gardner has given us a model and a vocabulary for exploring these skills as part of the education process. The significance of this model should not be overlooked, because before we can begin to solve problems we must have a common vocabulary to communicate. Without a proper vocabulary, it is impossible to see and make sense of patterns or relationships; without adequate terminology, a student who continues to make the same mistakes is simply "not trying." But with the right vocabulary we can talk about the student's lack of intrapersonal intelligence and begin to work on developing it so that he can learn from his mistakes. Put another way, "Only when data have been assigned meaning do they become useful information" (Conner, 1998, p. 20).

The public's enthusiasm for Daniel Goleman's work on emotional intelligence only serves to reinforce the importance of the personal intelligences.

That said, in many schools the step to formally address the personal intelligences through curriculum and in assessment remains a big one. Here, as in many other areas, I believe that education will follow the lead taken by business. A spate of books and articles about emotional intelligence (Gardner's personal intelligences) in the workplace can be found on bookstore shelves and in journal articles. As businesses become cognizant about the important role that the personal intelligences play in organizational success, the need for schools to prepare students appropriately becomes clearer and the push for appropriate instruction louder. As a consequence, more educators will begin to see that they have a responsibility for helping students develop their personal intelligences.

The Teacher's Role and MI

Along with seeing MI as a way to help more students succeed, the other reason that educators have been so receptive to the theory is that it validates their role as professionals. Using MI is at the other end of the spectrum from working with "teacher-proof" materials that direct teachers' every action. Using MI is also a way to respond to the continued "dumbing down" of textbooks. Teachers who use MI develop curriculum and assessment tools and are creative in their pedagogy. And teachers who use MI usually do so with others, working and learning as colleagues. In this way, implementing MI becomes a route to developing or extending professionalism among teachers.

MI often works best in schools that embrace site-based management, where the decisions that affect the students and faculty at a particular school are made by those who work in that school. Whether the school is a charter school, independent or religious school, or a public school that has been granted significant autonomy, the best implementations of MI come about when an entire faculty can work collaboratively as professionals to fashion strategies that fit their school's context and culture.

Not a Quick Fix

Despite the many virtues of MI and the incredible enthusiasm with which educators have embraced it, real questions remain about how widely it will be used. Successfully implementing MI is challenging for many schools because it requires more time, energy, and creativity from teachers; new assessment tools and techniques; and a coordinated effort to educate parents. Using MI is challenging because it causes us to question many of the traditional assumptions we have held in looking at who is smart and what should be taught in schools.

Our strengths are our weaknesses, and it is these virtues that give me some concern about the future of MI in schools. Unfortunately, in education we often veer to solutions that are simple, quick, and easy— attributes that don't describe the use of MI in any school. As I look to the future, then, I do not envision MI school systems, an abolition of standardized tests and traditional report cards, or textbook companies going out of business. And that may be OK. The test of the merit of MI should not be how many teachers use it or in how many schools it can be found. Although increased use of MI is desirable because it means more students can benefit from it, expecting it to be used pervasively is simply not realistic.

That said, the momentum of MI seems inexorable. When I look to the future, I see educators—a teacher here, a school there, a pocket of teachers in this school, a group of schools in that district—understanding that MI can be a tool that helps more children grow. Sure, bringing MI into the classroom can make our roles more professional and using it can help us grow and learn with our colleagues. But most important—and most exciting—using MI gives us more ways to help our students learn.

AFTERWORD:
EXCELLENCE VERSUS
PERFECTION

Years ago at a principals' seminar, the topic for a Friday afternoon presentation was "How I relieve stress in my life." As you might imagine, the room was packed. I was on the panel with several other principals. Our task was to share our strategies for stress reduction. Several ideas were offered, from engaging in physical recreation to teaching graduate classes. Finally, the last panelist, a high school principal, began to speak. In a low voice he said, "I keep my stress manageable because *I recognize the difference between excellence and perfection.*" He paused and the room was suddenly alive. Every person edged forward in the chair and every person's eyes were riveted on the speaker. (I felt the same way and then thought, "Boy, I'm glad I'm not following him!")

He continued, "I believe it is important that my students bus their tables and put their trays away after they have eaten." At this there were looks of surprise, a few smiles, and even a guffaw or two. "Stop," he said with some indignation, "I'm serious." The room hushed again.

"You may think this is being nitpicky or that it's a minor issue, but it's not. I believe that teaching kids responsibility is maybe the most important lesson we offer. Plus, my students generally come from upper-income families and the cafeteria staff is largely minority. What's the message when they walk away and leave their trays, making others pick up after them?"

By now he had the audience's full attention again. "We talk about this and work at it and I can get 96 percent of my students to put their trays away. That's good, no, that's excellent. But it's not perfection! And I want 100 percent of the trays put away," he continued, his voice rising.

"But I've come to realize," he went on, "that by striving for 100 percent, by pushing to get perfection, I turn the place into a prison. Students, faculty, and staff are uncomfortable and the cafeteria isn't a pleasant place to be. And in doing this I create an incredible amount of stress for myself, not to mention everyone around me. *So I've learned to be satisfied with excellence.* You know, 96 percent of the trays being put away is excellent. It's just fine."

The room was quiet for several minutes. Of course, the point was much larger than putting away cafeteria trays. Each of us was lost in reverie, thinking of those situations in our own schools where we've pushed for perfection, where excellence just wasn't good enough. Like this principal, I'm sure, we were realizing that there is a cost that comes from striving to attain perfection, and that it isn't always worthwhile to push beyond excellence.

When I returned to school on Monday I convened my administrative team and told them this story. It had the same powerful effect on them. We began to talk about issues on which we had fallen into the "excellence versus perfection" trap, being sucked into pushing harder and further, seeking the

PERFECT solution. Alas, there was no shortage of examples! I also shared this story with the faculty. Again, each of them could think of a time when they had crossed that line and the price of perfection was too high.

I have shared this story of excellence versus perfection many times in lots of different settings. It applies not just to schools but to organizations of all kinds and even to personal relationships. Yet I find it particularly relevant when thinking about the evolution of an MI school. Because there is no one, right way of implementing MI, whatever is being done can be done better. Or it can be done more efficiently. Or it can be done better and more efficiently! The list of possibilities is endless—and by definition, perfection can never be realized. As a result, frustration and stress can become perpetual handmaidens in the MI journey. After all, while it is possible to get all of the cafeteria trays put away, it is not possible to realize perfection in implementing MI. The MI journey is an endless one. As we contemplate ways in which MI can be used to help students learn, we need to consciously remember that there is no perfect destination, that the best we can hope for is a journey of excellence.

Appendix A

MI Inventory

Use this inventory as a tool to facilitate discussion about MI. Faculty members may use this inventory to reflect on their personal MI profile as well as how MI-friendly they make their classrooms.

PERSONAL INVENTORY

1. What intelligence(s) do you use to relax? Circle those that you use in your spare time.

LINGUISTIC   LOGICAL-MATHEMATICAL   SPATIAL   MUSICAL

BODILY-KINESTHETIC   NATURALIST   INTERPERSONAL   INTRAPERSONAL

2. Write yes or no after each of the following questions.

Do you enjoy learning new words?

Does learning a musical instrument come easily to you?

Do you notice architectural details?

Do you balance your checkbook?

Do you often find yourself making the same mistake?

Can you name the kinds of trees on the block where you live?

Are you physically active? Do you exercise regularly or play a recreational sport?

Do you have the music on when you drive, work, or read?

Do you write letters to people who live in town?

Do you like to spend time alone, thinking and reflecting?

Do you have a hobby that requires skill with your hands, like knitting or woodworking?

Do you have hobbies in which you create art?

Are you someone to whom others turn for advice?

Do you prepare your own taxes?

Is spending time outdoors something you value?

Do you find things boring unless there are others around?

3. If you are at a lecture, what would be most likely to help you remember the content?

Use numbers to indicate preference, 1 = most likely, 5 = least likely.

    a. If you take notes by hand or on a laptop computer _____

    b. If you draw a mind-map _____

    c. If you doodle, drawing images while listening _____

    d. If you talk with someone immediately afterward to share what is said _____

    e. If you create a mnemonic device to capture the main points _____

4. When giving someone who is new to town directions to a restaurant, you would

    a. Draw a map _____

    b. Write a narrative description _____

    c. Explain using lots of hand gestures _____

    d. Have them call the restaurant and ask how to get there _____

CLASSROOM INVENTORY

1. Write the initials of the 3 smartest students in your class(es) this year: _____, _____, _____.
What makes them smart?

2. Think over the past week of your teaching. In your lessons, how often have students been able to use the following intelligences to gain or learn information:

	Never	1–3 or more	4 or more
linguistic			
logical-mathematical			
spatial			
musical			
bodily-kinesthetic			
naturalist			
interpersonal			
intrapersonal			

3. Think over the past week of your teaching. In your lessons, how often have students been able to use the following intelligences to share or report information:

	None	1–3	4 or more
linguistic			
logical-mathematical			
spatial			
musical			.
bodily-kinesthetic			
naturalist			
interpersonal			
intrapersonal			

4. When you report student progress to parents, either in a report card, at a parent-teacher conference, or by the work that you send home to be perused, which intelligences are reflected?

	Rarely	Sometimes	Often
linguistic			
logical-mathematical			
spatial			
musical			
bodily-kinesthetic			
naturalist			
interpersonal			
intrapersonal			

5. How often are students given options, ways to use different intelligences, to complete an assignment?

	Rarely	Sometimes	Often
linguistic			
logical-mathematical			
spatial			
musical			
bodily-kinesthetic			
naturalist			
interpersonal			
intrapersonal			

6. Considering your answers to these questions, students with which intelligences are most likely to succeed in your classroom?

APPENDIX B

Sample Progress Report

NEW CITY SCHOOL • 5209 Waterman Avenue • St. Louis, MO 63108
5th Grade PROGRESS REPORT

Name _____

Attendance: Absent _____ Tardy _____

Teachers: _____

Key: ED	=	EXCEEDING DEVELOPMENTAL EXPECTATIONS
DA	=	DEVELOPING APPROPRIATELY
AC	=	AREA OF CONCERN
#	=	NEEDS ADDED ATTENTION

INTRAPERSONAL DEVELOPMENT Can self-assess; understands and shares own feelings	Reporting Period: 1	2
I. CONFIDENCE • Is comfortable taking a position different from the peer group • Engages in appropriate risk-taking behaviors • Is comfortable in both leader and follower roles • Copes with frustrations and failures • Demonstrates a positive and accurate self-concept		
II. MOTIVATION • Demonstrates internal motivation • Is actively involved in the learning process • Shows curiosity • Shows tenacity • Exhibits creativity		
III. PROBLEM SOLVING • Shows good judgment • Asks for help when needed • Can generate possible hypotheses and solutions • Shows perseverance in solving problems • Accepts and learns from feedback		
IV. RESPONSIBILITY • Accepts responsibility for own actions, practices self-control • Accepts responsibility for materials and belongings • Handles transitions and changes well • Accepts limits in work and play situations • Uses an appropriate sense of humor		
V. EFFORT AND WORK HABITS • Participates in activities and discussions • Works through assignments and activities carefully and thoroughly • Keeps notebook, desk, and locker/cubby organized • Completes homework assignments on time • Has age-appropriate attention span • Works independently • Follows written and oral directions • Listens attentively • Proofreads carefully • Uses time effectively		

NEW CITY SCHOOL • 5209 Waterman Avenue • St. Louis, MO 63108
5th Grade PROGRESS REPORT

INTERPERSONAL DEVELOPMENT Can successfully interact with others	Reporting Period:	
	1	2
I. APPRECIATION FOR DIVERSITY		
• Makes decisions based on appropriate information, rather than stereotypes		
• Understands the perspectives of others, including those of other races and cultures		
• Shows concern and empathy for others		
• Respects the individuality of others		
II. TEAMWORK		
• Cooperates with peers and adults		
• Works at conflict resolution		
• Behaves responsibly in groups		
• Demonstrates an ability to compromise		
• Expresses feelings and gives feedback constructively and appropriately		

COMMENTS:

Name _____   **LINGUISTIC INTELLIGENCE**

5th Grade   / = Not assessed
☐ Fall   ☐ Spring   at this time

EXPRESSIVE LANGUAGE—ORAL

	Fall Expectations	Spring Expectations	

PRESENTATION Goal: to communicate information clearly	Not Yet	Developing	Achieving	Extending
	• does not use appropriate volume, and presentation is difficult to hear • does not use visual aids when they are required, or uses aids of poor quality • looks away from audience or down at paper • exhibits little understanding of topic • lacks preparation and/or organization • ideas are difficult to follow • is uncomfortable in front of audience	• uses appropriate volume some of the time • uses visual aids some of the time • makes eye contact intermittently • sometimes exhibits clear understanding of topic • sometimes shows preparation and/or organization • progression of ideas lacks continuity • is beginning to exhibit poise	• projects clear speaking voice • uses relevant visual aids effectively • maintains eye contact • exhibits clear understanding of topic • shows preparation and organization • demonstrates fluid progression of ideas • exhibits poise with peers	• engages and holds auidence through voice level and expression • enriches the presentation with visual aids • engages and holds audience through eye contact • makes complex issue understandable • information presented is concise and pertinent • fields questions from the audience with ease • is poised with nonpeer groups

NY	D	A	E

EXPRESSIVE LANGUAGE—WRITTEN

MECHANICS Goal: to communicate effectively in written form	Not Yet	Developing	Achieving	Extending
	• does not understand sentence structure • rarely writes in paragraph form, which includes indenting, writing a topic sentence and writing supporting details • uses correct capitalization including for geographic regions and countries • makes frequent errors in punctuation • has multiple spelling errors including 5th grade core words • cannot edit • does not understand what a thesis statement is	• writes in complete sentences but has frequent run-on sentences • writes in paragraph form, which includes indenting, writing a topic sentence and writing supporting details • uses proper capitalization • uses correct punctuation at the end of a sentence, commas in a series and in compound sentences, and uses correct punctuation in dialogue • spells with few errors in daily work • misses some errors when editing • is able to construct a thesis statement with assistance for the purpose of essay writing	• writes in complete sentences with varied sentence structure • writes well-developed paragraphs (indenting, topic sentence and supporting details) • uses correct capitalization consistently • demonstrates an understanding of the proper use of colons and semi-colons • is able to incorporate spelling and vocabulary words in his/her writing • edits for mechanics/proofreads with few mistakes • is able to construct a thesis statement for the purpose of essay writing	• able to utilize different writing styles • uses transition sentences to connect paragraphs • uses a variety of punctuation regularly and correctly to produce a particular style • searches for and uses new vocabulary in language and writing • edits in a way not only to correct but to enhance written work • shows clear relationships between introduction, body and closing in written pieces

NY	D	A	E

Name _____ **LINGUISTIC INTELLIGENCE**

5th Grade

☐ Fall   ☐ Spring

/ = Not assessed
at this time

PROGRESSIVE LANGUAGE—WRITTEN

	Fall Expectations		Spring Expectations	
CONTENT Goal: to communicate ideas effectively in various forms	**Not Yet**	**Developing**	**Achieving**	**Extending**
	• rarely responds to feedback on written work by making appropriate changes • rarely conveys ideas clearly for varied purposes (business letter, essay, short story) • rarely supports thesis statement with appropriate and logical details • does not incorporate details, dialogue and similes to expland writing • rarely edits for clarity	• sometimes responds to feedback on written work by making appropriate changes • sometimes conveys ideas clearly for varied purposes • incorporates logical and appropriate details in creative and essay writing • sometimes edits for clarity	• responds to feedback on written work by making appropriate changes • conveys ideas clearly for varied purposes (business letter, essay, short story) • supports thesis statement with appropriate and logical details • writes creatively using details, dialogue and similes • edits for clarity	• initiates feedback from peers and adults • thesis statement is supported logically, thoroughly and creatively • uses an extensive repertoire of techniques to expand writing • after editing, writing is clear and precise

NY	D	A	E

RECEPTIVE LANGUAGE—READING

COMPREHENSION Goal: to understand what has been read using age-appopriate materials	**Not Yet**	**Developing**	**Achieving**	**Extending**
	• rarely notes supporting details • makes literal interpretations • recounts details but is unable to identify main idea	• identifies supporting details • makes inferences/draws realistic conclusions with prompting • has difficulty summarizing the main idea	• consistently identifies supporting details • makes inferences/draws realistic conclusions • summarizes the main idea	• compares supporting details from various stories to help illustrate a point • uses analogies to illustrate inferences and conclusions • summarizes the main idea when it is not clearly stated

NY	D	A	E

LITERARY TECHNIQUES Goal: to identify literary elements in context effectively	**Not Yet**	**Developing**	**Achieving**	**Extending**
	• is unable to identify literary elements in context	• occasionally identifies literary elements in context	• consistently identifies literary elements in context	• transfers literary elements to other disciplines

NY	D	A	E

Name _____   **LINGUISTIC INTELLIGENCE**

5th Grade

☐ Fall   ☐ Spring

/ = Not assessed
at this time

STUDY SKILLS Goal: to use resources effectively	Not Yet	Developing	Achieving	Extending
	• does not use initiative or has no idea where to go to locate needed information • cannot take notes	• asks where to go to locate needed information • tends to copy information directly from sources	• obtains useful information from a wide variety of sources • takes notes and completes an outline independently	• takes initiative to locate and share information • takes notes and uses a variety of outlines to independently organize thoughts

NY	D	A	E

COMMENTS:

Effort in developing Linguistic Intelligence: READING: AC   DA   ED

WRITING: AC   DA   ED

AC = Area of Concern

DA = Developing Appropriately

ED = Exceeding Developmental Expectations

_____

Teacher

Name _____   **LOGICAL-MATHEMATICAL INTELLIGENCE**

5th Grade

☐ Fall   ☐ Spring

/ = Not assessed
at this time

	Fall Expectations		Spring Expectations	
NUMBER AND COMPUTATION CONCEPTS Goal: to exhibit practical and conceptual understanding of numbers and computation	**Not Yet**	**Developing**	**Achieving**	**Extending**
	• does not know multiplication and division facts to 144 • inconsistently multiplies a 3-digit number by a 2-digit number, or divides with a 2-digit divisor • does not understand the concept of adding and subtracting fractions with unlike denominators • inconsistently multiplies and divides fractions • inconsistently adds and subtracts decimals • does not understand the relationship between fractions and decimals • sees no relationships between percents and fractions/decimals • does not understand the concept of prime numbers • does not understand square numbers and other powers	• knows multiplication and division facts to 144 but cannot meet time standard • multiplies a 2- and 3-digit number by a 2-digit number, and divides with a 2-digit divisor with a model • using a model, adds, subtracts and compares fractions with unlike denominators, proper and improper fractions, mixed numbers • multiplies and divides fractions using a model • adds and subtracts decimals, and inconsistently multiplies and divides decimals • converts fractions to and from decimals using a model • explores the concept of percent in relationship to fractions/decimals • begins to develop an understanding of prime numbers and prime factorization • begins to show an understanding of square numbers and other powers	• knows multiplication and division facts to 144 with speed and accuracy • multiplies a 3-digit number by a 2-digit number, and divides with a 2-digit divisor with accuracy • adds, subtracts and compares fractions with unlike denominators, proper and improper fractions, mixed numbers • begins to demonstrate understanding of multiplying and dividing fractions • adds, subtracts, multiplies and divides decimals • begins to convert fractions and decimals independently • begins to understand the concept of percent in relationship to fractions/ decimals	• knows multiplication and division facts to 144 with speed and accuracy (more than 36/minute) • multiplies and divides whole numbers with multiple digits accurately • adds and subtracts fractions and mixed numbers with unlike denominators to solve problems in the real world • multiplies and divides fractions/mixed numbers accurately • adds, subtracts, multiplies and divides decimals to solve problems in the real world • interchanges fractions and decimals • interprets percent as a means of comparison of quantities of different sizes, and as a rate of change • understands prime numbers and prime factorization • understands powers

NY	D	A	E

STATISTICS Goal: to exhibit practical and conceptual understanding of statistics	**Not Yet**	**Developing**	**Achieving**	**Extending**
	• does not understand what is measurable • cannot create/interpret statistical information • solves problems that involve collecting and analyzing data with assistance • cannot recognize statistical terms	• collects, organizes and describes data in various forms (tables, charts and graphs) with assistance • constructs, reads and interprets displays of data with a model • solves problems that involve collecting and analyzing simple data • recognizes statistical terms	• collects, organizes and describes data in various forms (tables, charts and graphs) • constructs, reads and interprets displays of data • formulates and solves problems that involve collecting and analyzing data • demonstrates an understanding of statistical terms (means, median, mode) on teacher-created projects	• collects, organizes, and analyzes complex data • constructs, reads and interprets displays of complex data • initiates and recognizes the usefulness of statistics in everyday life • manipulates data

NY	D	A	E

Name _____ **LOGICAL-MATHEMATICAL INTELLIGENCE**

5th Grade

☐ Fall ☐ Spring

/ = Not assessed
at this time

	Fall Expectations	Spring Expectations	
GEOMETRY AND MEASUREMENT Goal: to exhibit practical and conceptual understanding of geometry and measurement	**Not Yet**	**Developing**	**Achieving**	**Extending**

NY	D	A	E

Not Yet	**Developing**	**Achieving**	**Extending**
• attempts to determine the surface area of 2-dimensional objects • calculates perimeter and circumference inaccurately • rarely identifies acute, obtuse and right angles • chooses inappropriate tools for measuring surface area, mass and volume • identifies some polygons • does not recognize symmetry, congruency and similarity	• determines the surface area of 2-dimensional objects accurately • calculates perimeter and circumference with direction • sometimes identifies acute, obtuse and right angles • chooses appropriate tools for measuring surface area, mass and volume with direction • identifies, describes and compares some polygons • recognizes symmetry, congruency and similarity • identifies line segment, ray and line	• determines the surface area of 2-dimensional objects and rectangular prisms accurately • calculates perimeter and circumference • identifies acute, obtuse and right angles • effectively uses appropriate tools for measuring surface area, mass and volume • identifies, describes and compares polygons • identifies and creates symmetry, congruency and similarity • identifies and creates line segment, ray and line	• identifies, compares and classifies 3-dimensional figures (prisms, pyramids, polyhedra) • uses perimeter and circumference to solve problems • uses a protractor to create acute, obtuse and right angles • is comfortable using tools to explore new situations • identifies polygons and understands the relationship between them (a square is a rhombus, a rectangle, a quadrilateral, a parallelogram, and a polygon • understands symmetry and explores transformations of geometric figures • transfers concepts to other areas

COMMENTS:

Effort in developing Logical-Mathematical Intelligence: AC   DA   ED

AC = Area of Concern

DA = Developing Appropriately

ED = Exceeding Developmental Expectations

_____
Teacher

91

New City School PERFORMING ARTS Progress Report

Grade _____5th_____   Teacher: **Diane Davenport**

Name _____   Date: ___December 1997___

Theme:

Making Connections is the theme in Performing Arts this year. Many of the intelligences are used in exploring the elements that connect the arts disciplines of creative movement, drama and music.

The students are involved in experiences related to the concept of expression. Music, drama and creative movement are modes of expression. Many of the intelligences are used as the students explore different types of theater. The students are preparing for performances of *Sneetches* and *Romeo and Juliet*. The students have also viewed performances of live theater.

INTRAPERSONAL DEVELOPMENT *Can self-assess; understands and shares own feelings*		SKILLS ASSESSMENT **This skill has been introduced but not assessed at this time.*	
CONFIDENCE Engages in appropriate risk-taking behaviors.		MUSIC Is able to sing songs in harmony.	
MOTIVATION Is actively involved in the learning process.		Is able to read two-part rhythm scores.	
PROBLEM SOLVING Shows good judgment.		Is able to identify complex differences in tempo, rhythm and melody.	
RESPONSIBILITY Accepts responsibility for own actions and materials.		CREATIVE MOVEMENT Demonstrates tension and relaxation.	
EFFORT and WORK HABITS Follows written and oral directions.		"Warms up" appropriately for dance and movement activities.	
INTERPERSONAL DEVELOPMENT *Can successfully interact with others.*		DRAMA Demonstrates awareness encounters.	
APPRECIATION FOR DIVERSITY Respects the individuality of others.		Can re-enact a scene or story, changing it in some way.	
TEAMWORK Cooperates with peers and adults.			

Key: AC = Area of Concern • DA = Developing Appropriately • ED = Exceeding Developmental Expectations
= Needs Added Attention

New City School BODILY-KINESTHETIC/PHYSICAL EDUCATION
Progress Report

Grade _____5th_____   Teacher: <u>Lauren McKenna</u>

Name _____   Date: _____May 1998_____

Theme:
The Bodily-Kinesthetic program will help students acquire the skills, knowledge and motivation to incorporate physical activity into their daily lives.

INTRAPERSONAL DEVELOPMENT		SKILLS ASSESSMENT
Can self-assess; understands and shares own feelings		**This skill has been introduced but not assessed at this time.*
CONFIDENCE Engages in appropriate risk-taking behaviors.		Number of Pull-ups at one time:
MOTIVATION Is actively involved in the learning process.		Number of Chin-ups at one time:
PROBLEM SOLVING Shows good judgment.		Flex Arm Hang: min. sec.
RESPONSIBILITY Accepts responsibility for own actions and materials.		Flex Chin Hang: min. sec
EFFORT and WORK HABITS Follows written and oral directions.		Mile Time: min. sec.
INTERPERSONAL DEVELOPMENT *Can successfully interact with others.*		
APPRECIATION FOR DIVERSITY Respects the individuality of others.		
TEAMWORK Cooperates with peers and adults.		

Key: AC = Area of Concern • DA = Developing Appropriately • ED = Exceeding Developmental Expectations
= Needs Added Attention

New City School LIBRARY Progress Report

Grade _____5th_____

Name _____

Teacher: <u>Nancy Solodar</u>

Date: _____May 1998_____

Theme:

The goals of the library program are threefold: to foster curiosity and a love of books and reading; to teach information literacy; and, to promote the growth and development of each child's sense of personal responsibility. A wide variety of reading material from various cultures and disciplines is available to students for leisure reading and research. Library skills are taught to enable the students to access print and non-print materials, evaluate these materials, and draw conclusions.

The fourth grade students have been working intensively on their library skills with special emphasis on how to use the card catalog, almanac, specialty dictionaries and atlases. Effective and efficient use of reference sources requires problem-solving skills and the determination to follow through. Lots of practice is needed before these skills, which are so necessary for future school work, are mastered. The students will continue to improve their research skills in 5th and 6th grade.

INTRAPERSONAL DEVELOPMENT *Can self-assess; understands and shares own feelings*		SKILLS ASSESSMENT *This skill has been introduced but not assessed at this time.*	
CONFIDENCE Engages in appropriate risk-taking behaviors.		Respects library materials and equipment.	
MOTIVATION Is actively involved in the learning process.		Shows respect for opinions and ideas of classmates.	
PROBLEM SOLVING Shows good judgment.		Uses the card catalog.	
RESPONSIBILITY Accepts responsibility for own actions and materials.		Uses the almanac.	
EFFORT and WORK HABITS Follows written and oral directions.		Uses the atlas.	
INTERPERSONAL DEVELOPMENT *Can successfully interact with others.*		Uses specialty dictionaries.	
APPRECIATION FOR DIVERSITY Respects the individuality of others.		Uses non-print reference materials.	
TEAMWORK Cooperates with peers and adults.			

Key: AC = Area of Concern • DA = Developing Appropriately • ED = Exceeding Developmental Expectations
= Needs Added Attention

New City School ART/SPATIAL Progress Report

Grade _____5th_____   Teacher: Betsy Ward____
Name _____   Date: ____May 1998____

Theme:
The spatial theme for this year is THE BODY. Integral to both the conception and execution of art since the dawn of creative expression, the human body seemed an obvious and exciting focus for our art explorations.

INTRAPERSONAL DEVELOPMENT *Can self-assess; understands and shares own feelings*		SKILLS ASSESSMENT *This skill has been introduced but not assessed at this time.*	
CONFIDENCE Engages in appropriate risk-taking behaviors.		Responds to a variety of art resources.	
MOTIVATION Is actively involved in the learning process.		Exhibits knowledge of different artists and cultures.	
PROBLEM SOLVING Shows good judgment.		Uses art vocabulary effectively.	
RESPONSIBILITY Accepts responsibility for own actions and materials.		Offers and accepts ideas and criticisms in a positive/productive manner.	
EFFORT and WORK HABITS Follows written and oral directions.		Enthusiastically pursues 2- and 3- dimensional work.	
INTERPERSONAL DEVELOPMENT *Can successfully interact with others.*		Manipulates tools and mediums carefully and successfully.	
APPRECIATION FOR DIVERSITY Respects the individuality of others.		Shows originality and creativity in self-expression.	
TEAMWORK Cooperates with peers and adults.		Demonstrates initiative and responsibility for clean-up processes.	

Key: AC = Area of Concern • DA = Developing Appropriately • ED = Exceeding Developmental Expectations
= Needs Added Attention

New City School SCIENCE Progress Report

Grade _____5th_____   Teacher: Susie Burge____
Name _____   Date: _____May 1998_____

Theme:

Classification: Ordering the World Around Us. Our year-long goals are found in four areas: Content, Skills, Responsibility, and Diversity. In **content**, we will be studying classification of plants and animals, laws of motion and energy, and geology. In **skills**, we will be learning and using science process skills and classroom study skills. Students will learn to take **responsibility** for their own learning and will also learn about **people** who have made contributions to science.

The fifth graders have been studying physics and geology this spring. The students learned about Newton's laws of motion as they designed their own race cars from milk cartons. They had to manipulate only one variable at a time as they experimented, measured and averaged their results. From energy of motion they moved to electrical energy. They built parallel and series circuits, and incorporated them into their own model houses.

In geology, they have studied the interior of the earth, continental drift theory, volcanoes and earthquakes. The students have obtained information from the Internet about daily earthquake occurrences, and plotted them on maps using latitude and longitude. They learned about forces shaping landforms, and used flowcharts to identify rocks.

INTRAPERSONAL DEVELOPMENT *Can self-assess; understands and shares own feelings*		SKILLS ASSESSMENT *This skill has been introduced but not assessed at this time.*	
CONFIDENCE Engages in appropriate risk-taking behaviors.		Can compare and contrast.	
MOTIVATION Is actively involved in the learning process.		Classifies.	
PROBLEM SOLVING Shows good judgment.		Records data accurately.	
RESPONSIBILITY Accepts responsibility for own actions and materials.		Creates and reads graphs.	
EFFORT and WORK HABITS Follows written and oral directions.		Takes notes in outline form.	
INTERPERSONAL DEVELOPMENT *Can successfully interact with others.*		Comes to class prepared.	
APPRECIATION FOR DIVERSITY Respects the individuality of others.		Uses equipment appropriately.	
TEAMWORK Cooperates with peers and adults.		Homework completed on time: _____ % Average homework score: _____ % Test and quiz average: _____ %	

Key: AC = Area of Concern • DA = Developing Appropriately • ED = Exceeding Developmental Expectations
= Needs Added Attention

New City School SPANISH/ESPANOL Progress Report

Grade _____5th_____   Teacher: <u>Zully Kuster</u>
Name _____   Date: _____May 1999_____

Theme:
This semester we delved deeply into a study of the country of Uruguay and the Uruguayan culture. We cooked some typical dishes, such as *scones* (biscuits) and *tortas fritas* (fried bread), while exploring some other traditions, such as drinking *mate* (herbal tea). A major focus of this theme study was for the students to learn that although our cultures are different in many ways, they are alike in so many other ways.

As part of our theme study we watched a video about Uruguay and read about the geography, economics and human resources of this country. The students also worked on projects ranging from cooking typical dishes to others that explained the patriymbols. We used these opportunities for the students to compare their life in the United States with one that a typical Uruguayan 6th grader would experience.

In addition to this focus on Uruguay, the students also explored the Spanish language learning vocabulary related to sports, time, feelings, and different stores in which they might shop.

INTRAPERSONAL DEVELOPMENT *Can self-assess; understands and shares own feelings*		**SKILLS ASSESSMENT** **This skill has been introduced but not assessed at this time.*	
CONFIDENCE Engages in appropriate risk-taking behaviors.		Exhibits knowledge of Spanish-speaking cultures introduced in class.	
MOTIVATION Is actively involved in the learning process.		Shows interest in learning Spanish.	
PROBLEM SOLVING Shows good judgment.		Exhibits knowledge of vocabulary.	
RESPONSIBILITY Accepts responsibility for own actions and materials.			
EFFORT and WORK HABITS Follows written and oral directions.			
INTERPERSONAL DEVELOPMENT *Can successfully interact with others.*			
APPRECIATION FOR DIVERSITY Respects the individuality of others.			
TEAMWORK Cooperates with peers and adults.			

Key: AC = Area of Concern • DA = Developing Appropriately • ED = Exceeding Developmental Expectations
= Needs Added Attention

Appendix C

Sample Worksheets

This appendix contains several worksheets you may wish to consider as you work through implementing MI.

End-of-Year Questionnaire

Directions

1. Turn the tape recorder on. Press PLAY and RECORD at the same time.

2. Say your name and today's date.

3. Read each question aloud and answer it as honestly and completely as you can. Remember to speak clearly and answer all parts of each question.

1. What do you think is the most important math skill you learned this year? Why do you think it's most important?

2. What do you think is the least important math skill you learned this year? Why do you think it's least important?

3. In what areas have you shown the most growth this year? Explain.

4. What math skills do you hope to continue to improve next year? Explain.

5. What have you learned about yourself as a mathematician this year? Explain.

Portfolio Peek

Name: _____ Date: _____

Before you open your portfolio, how do you feel about portfolios?

_____

_____

Open your portfolio. Look through the contents. Enjoy your work. Then answer these questions.

1. What do you notice about your portfolio?

_____

_____

2. Is there any intelligence represented with more samples than another intelligence?
List the intelligences that have the most samples.

_____

_____

3. What do you think this means about you?

_____

_____

4. Are there any intelligences for which you do not have any samples in your portfolio? List these intelligences.

_____

_____

5. What new insights do you have about yourself?

_____

_____

Progress Report Reflection

Name: _____ Date: _____

1. What two areas have improved since the first grading period?

_____

_____

Why? _____

2. What two areas do you want to work on for the next three months?

_____

_____

Why? _____

3. What would be a good topic for me to discuss with your parents at our conference?

_____

_____

Because? _____

4. What is something you want to accomplish before the end of this year to be ready for the next grade?

_____

_____

Because? _____

Presentation Reflection

Name: _____ Date: _____

Your presentation will be judged on the following criteria:

_____ Spoke loudly and clearly
_____ Made eye contact with the audience
_____ Showed poise and used self control
_____ Presented accurate information using note cards
_____ Used two to five minutes for the presentation

Think about this information as you watch the videotape of your presentation. Then complete the following sections.

A. List three things you did well during your presentation.
1. _____
2. _____
3. _____

B. List three areas you want to improve during your next opportunity to give a presentation.
1. _____
2. _____
3. _____

C. Give one strategy that you will use to help yourself make these improvements.

_____
_____

Working with a Partner

Name: _____ Date: _____

Circle the answer that best answers each statement.

1. My partner and I worked well together.	Always	Sometimes	Never
2. We both shared ideas.	Always	Sometimes	Never
3. We tried to solve problems.	Always	Sometimes	Never
4. We used good effort.	Always	Sometimes	Never
5. We are proud of the work we did.	Always	Sometimes	Never

Write a sentence or two to fill out the following statements.

6. Here's an example of something we did well:

_____

_____

_____

_____

7. Here's an example of something we will work on the next time we have partners:

_____

_____

_____

_____

How Are We Doing?

Group: _____ Date: _____

Give two examples for each statement.

1. We each contributed ideas _____ often, _____ sometimes, _____ not very much.

2. We listened to each other _____ often, _____ sometimes, _____ not very much.

3. We encouraged each other _____ often, _____ sometimes, _____ not very much.

4. We built on each other's ideas _____ often, _____ sometimes, _____ not very much.

APPENDIX D

Spring Parent Survey

Dear Parents,

Children learn best when the school and home work together. An important part of that working together, that partnership, is two-way communication. New City does, I think, a good job of communicating *to* you: You receive weekly letters from your child's teachers and from me, there are newsletters and annual reports, along with other mailings. In addition, our halls and walls abound with samples of student work and information for you.

But, as good as it is, that is **one-way communication,** us to you.

For our children to learn best, we need to hear from you. That already happens in a variety of ways, but each year I try to formally capture your feelings and thoughts: What do you value most at New City? In what areas do we need improvement?

It is very important that you take the time to share your thoughts with us. Even if you have done this ten (!) times before, your thoughts are important. To facilitate your response, we have enclosed a self-addressed, stamped envelope. Please complete and return this survey by June 1. If you have more than one child at New City, please return a survey for each child as their experiences will be somewhat different. If you choose to return only one survey (for multiple children), please indicate the various grade levels of your children. And, of course, please indicate if you would like a personal response from me.

In advance, thank you for your thoughts!

Sincerely,

Thomas R. Hoerr, Ph.D.
Director
trhoerr@newcityschool.org, TRHoerr@aol.com

Spring Parent Survey

Please return by June 1

Name (optional)_____

Check here _____ if you would like a personal response from Tom.

Child's grade: 3/4   4/5   5/6   6/7   7/8   8/9   4th   5th   6th

Including this year, how many years have you had 1 child or more at NCS? _____

1. Why are you at New City School? Please rank the reasons, 1 = most important.

   a. Strong academic program _____

   b. Focus on the personal intelligences, nurturing environment _____

   c. Family Support program _____

   d. Valuing of racial and socioeconomic diversity _____

   e. NCS location _____

   f. Lower cost than most other independent schools _____

   g. Other factors? Please list and prioritize:

   _____   _____

   _____   _____

2. Which of the factors listed in question 1 are essential? Place a star by each factor that you consider essential in your choosing NCS.

3. Please give three words that describe the strengths of NCS.

4. Please give three words that describe the weaknesses of NCS.

Please circle the response that most closely captures your feelings. Narrative comments and clarifications are always welcome!

5. My child's individual needs have been met.	strongly agree	agree	disagree	strongly disagree
6. Tom has been friendly and supportive.	strongly agree	agree	disagree	strongly disagree
7. I understand how the use of multiple intelligence theory helps my child.	strongly agree	agree	disagree	strongly disagree

Please share your thoughts with me.

8. If you could change one thing about NCS, what would it be?

9. Other thoughts, questions, or observations?

RESOURCES

Many web sites contain information about MI. A particularly interesting web site is Harvard Project Zero's Project SUMIT (Schools Using Multiple Intelligence Theory), directed by Mindy Kornhaber http://pzweb.harvard.edu/sumit. The site features a compilation of schools using MI and it also lists more than 40 schools using MI in different ways. Other web sites that I recommend are the Project Zero web site http://pzweb.harvard.edu/ and www.newhorizons.org. The web site http://www.ascd.org/pubs/el/sept97/sept97.html features the multiple intelligences theme issue of *Educational Leadership*.

In addition to the books listed in the References section of this book, I would also recommend *Discovering the Naturalist Intelligence* by Jenna Glock, Susan Wertz, and Maggie Meyer (Tucson, AZ: Zephyr Press, 1999), *Teaching and Learning Through Multiple Intelligences* by Bruce Campbell, Linda Campbell, and Dee Dickenson (Needham, Heights, MA: Allyn & Bacon, 1996) and *Seven Pathways of Learning: Teaching Students and Parents About Multiple Intelligences* by David Lazear (Tucson, AZ: Zephyr Press, 1994). Also, Gardner's 1993 book, *Multiple Intelligences: The Theory in Practice* (New York: Basic Books) is worth reading.

I also highly recommend his newest book, *The Disciplined Mind* (New York: Simon & Schuster, 1999). More pragmatic than his previous works, in this book he specifically looks at how curriculum and instruction should address students' understanding of truth, goodness, and beauty. Gardner revisits MI in *Intelligence Reframed: Multiple Intelligences in the 21st Century*, a book scheduled to be published in fall 1999.

In addition, I would be remiss if I did not mention the two books created by the New City School faculty: *Celebrating Multiple Intelligences* (St. Louis, MO: 1994) and *Succeeding with Multiple Intelligences* (St. Louis, MO: 1996).

As the facilitator of the ASCD Multiple Intelligences Network, I have heard from thousands of educators who are either interested in using MI or are using MI. Hundreds of educators travel from around the country, sometimes from around the world, to visit New City School each year (more than 700 educators came to see us in the 1998–99 school year). We have hosted three MI conferences, attracting people from across the country and our faculty has sold thousands of books about our work with MI. For more information on the ASCD Multiple Intelligences Network, to arrange visit, or to ask a question, contact me at trhoerr@newcityschool.org or trhoerr@AOL.com.

REFERENCES

Adizes, I. (1988). *Corporate lifecyles.* Englewood, NJ: Prentice Hall.

Angelou, M. (1970). *I know why the caged bird sings.* New York: Random House.

Armstrong, T. (1994). *Multiple intelligences in the classroom.* Alexandria, VA: ASCD.

Barth, R. (1990). *Improving schools from within.* San Francisco, CA: Jossey-Bass.

Beals, M. (1994). *Warriors don't cry.* New York: Pocket Books.

Bennis, W. (1997). *Managing people is like herding cats.* Provo, UT: Executive Excellence Publishing.

Blythe, T. (1998). *The teaching for understanding guide.* San Francisco, CA: Jossey-Bass.

Bridges, W. (1991). *Managing transitions.* Reading, MA: Persus Books.

Coles, R. (1997). *The moral intelligence of children.* New York: Penguin Group.

Conner, D. (1998). *Leading at the edge of chaos.* New York: John Wiley & Sons.

Csikszentmihalyi, M. (1990). *Flow: The psychology of optimal experience.* New York: Harper & Row.

De Paoloa, T. (1978). *The popcorn book.* New York: Holiday House.

Dyson, E. (1998). *Release 2.1.* New York: Broadway Books.

Early, G. (1994). *Daughters.* Reading, MA: Addison Wesley.

Faculty of the New City School. (1994). *Celebrating multiple intelligences: Teaching for success.* St. Louis, MO: The New City School.

Faculty of the New City School. (1996). *Succeeding with multiple intelligences: Teaching through the personal intelligences.* St. Louis, MO: The New City School.

Fullan, M. (1990). Staff development, innovation, and institutional development. In B. Joyce (Ed.), *Changing school culture through staff development.* Alexandria, VA: ASCD.

Gardner, H. (1983). *Frames of mind: The theory of multiple intelligences.* New York: Basic Books.

Gardner, H. (1991). *The unschooled mind.* New York: Basic Books.

George, J. (1972). *Julie of the wolves.* New York: Harper Collins.

Goleman, D. (1995). *Emotional intelligence.* New York: Bantam Books.

Goleman, D. (1998). *Working with emotional intelligence.* New York: Bantam Books.

Goleman, D. (1998, November-December). What makes a leader? *Harvard Business Review 76*(6), 92–102.

Goodwin, D. (1994). *No ordinary times.* New York: Simon & Schuster.

Hallowell, E. (1999, January-February). The human moment at work. *Harvard Business Review 77*(1), 58–66.

Krechevsky, M., Gardner, H., & Hoerr., T. (1994). *Complimentary energies: Implementing MI theory from the lab and from the field.* In J. Oakes and K. H. Quartz (Eds.), *Creating new educational communities: Schools and classrooms where all children are smart.* National Society for the Study of Education Handbook

Lambert, L., Walker, D., Zimmerman, D., Cooper, J., Lambert, M., Gardner, M., Slack, P. (1995). *The constructivist leader.* New York: Teachers College Press.

Lightfoot, S. L. (1983). *The good high school.* New York: Basic Books.

McDonald, J. (1996). *Redesigning school.* San Francisco, CA: Jossey-Bass.

Moyers, B. (1989). *A world of ideas.* New York: Doubleday.

Paley, V. (1979). *White teacher.* Cambridge, MA: Harvard University Press.

Peters, T., & Waterman, R., Jr. (1982). *In search of excellence.* New York: Harper & Row.

Senge, P. (1990). *The fifth discipline.* New York: Doubleday.

Sternberg, R. (1988). *The triarchic mind.* New York: Viking.

Wiggins, G., & McTighe, J. (1998). *Understanding by design.* Alexandria, VA: ASCD.

ABOUT THE AUTHOR

Thomas R. Hoerr has been the director of the New City School in St. Louis, Missouri, since 1981. In 1988, the New City faculty began implementing the theory of multiple intelligences (MI). Hoerr has written extensively about the educational applications of the theory of multiple intelligences and the importance of collegiality, and he often presents these topics at schools and conferences. Prior to leading New City School, Hoerr taught in two school districts and was an elementary school principal in the school district of University City in St. Louis.

For 15 years Hoerr taught graduate-level courses to prospective school administrators. In addition, he designed, coordinated, and taught in the Management Program at Washington University in St. Louis. Hoerr describes his experience at Washington University as particularly rich because he was able to look at leadership and management in other sectors and in several profit and nonprofit organizations, and can apply the lessons to education. Hoerr holds a Ph.D. in Educational Policymaking and Planning from Washington University.

Hoerr can be contacted at New City School, 5209 Waterman Avenue, St. Louis, MO 63108 USA, or by e-mail at trhoerr@AOL.com or trhoerr@newcityschool.org.

Index

Page numbers followed by *f* indicate a reference to a figure, page numbers followed by *n* indicate a footnote.

thematic instruction, 12–13, 13*f*, 36–37
time, for student reflection, 45–48
Triarchic Theory of Intelligence, 3

University of Rio Grande, 75

values, personal intelligences and, 48, 51

weaknesses, recognition of, 9–10, 36, 43
web sites, 106
Wiggins, Grant, 74–75
Working with a Partner, 102–103
Working with Emotional Intelligence (Goleman), 48

Related ASCD Resources: Multiple Intelligences

***Becoming a Multiple Intelligences School* from the Books in Action Video Series**
In this video filmed at New City School, you'll see firsthand some of the effective practices described in the book *Becoming a Multiple Intelligences School,* including how multiple intelligences theory guides curriculum, instruction, assessment, the parent-teacher relationship, and teacher collaboration. Author and school director Thomas R. Hoerr takes you to classrooms and faculty meetings where teachers use multiple intelligences perspectives to plan lessons and improve student achievement. *Becoming a Multiple Intelligences School,* ASCD videotape, 15 minutes. Stock no. 400213

   Special Books-in-Action Bundle. Perfect for facilitating group discussion and learning. One videotape with 10 copies of the book *Becoming a Multiple Intelligences School.* Stock no. 700218

Audiotapes

Authentic Assessment Using the Multiple Intelligences

How Multiple Intelligences and Learning Style Fit: The Research and Practical Applications

Multiple Assessments for Multiple Intelligences by Beth Swartz

Multiple Intelligences—Putting a Theory into Practice by Helen Flamm, Connie Canter, Ernest Flamm, & Carolyn Wheeler

Multiple Intelligences Team Building and Class Building

On Multiple Intelligences and Education by Howard Gardner

Teaching for Understanding Through Multiple Intelligences by Geni Boyer

Teaching Thinking to Multiple Intelligences and Diverse Student Populations by Richard Strong

CD-ROMs

Exploring Our Multiple Intelligences

Online Courses

Multiple Intelligences Professional Development course

Print Products

ASCD Topic Pack—Multiple Intelligences

Multiple Intelligences and Student Achievement: Success Stories from Six Schools by Linda Campbell and Bruce Campbell

Multiple Intelligences in the Classroom by Thomas Armstrong

Videotapes

The Multiple Intelligences Series by Bruce and Linda Campbell

For more information, visit us on the World Wide Web (http://www.ascd.org), send an e-mail message to member@ascd.org, call the ASCD Service Center (1-800-933-ASCD or 703-578-9600, then press 2), send a fax to 703-575-5400, or write to Information Services, ASCD, 1703 N. Beauregard St., Alexandria, VA 22311-1714 USA.